In Praise of *Bouncing Back*

We are in times of change: the economy, glob... ...., ... its always the ones who are the most adaptable to change who will survive. In his latest book, Richard gives you a choice between staying stuck or bouncing back – and of course you want to bounce back. The book is full of tips and advice to help you to do so.

Richard gives you real insight into how he's transformed his life, and it is refreshing to read such honesty about his first-hand experience.

I am a huge fan of Richard's books and with this one I definitely feel he's captured the "shift" that is happening in the world right now, which has left many unsettled and for some has been like a turbulence. But change is good and *Bouncing Back* definitely gives you the tools to adapt.

Julie Bishop, Founder, www.jobhop.co.uk

Once again, Richard tackles a difficult change process with pragmatism, empathy and humour. When you wake up the morning after your sudden career change, it's all too easy to think, how did that happen, why me, and then – what now? Yesterday you had purpose, identity, structure, recognition... but what do you have today? Well, for a start, you have the rest of your life in front of you and time to think – and thinking time is working.

Once you reflect on what you have achieved you realise the grass really is green, the sky blue and the poppies red. Before that, you'd been so tied up in the job that it was difficult to actually see. Using practical examples and a clear structured approach, *Bouncing Back* really will help you bounce back – and bounce much higher than you did before.

David Clover, Chief Executive, Quadra-Foil Limited

Bouncing Back is a pragmatic, mildly irreverent and hugely enjoyable guide to surviving the inevitable knock-backs in our modern career. I've found it a fantastic insight and guide to the roller-coaster of emotions that I experienced when my role was made redundant. This book helped me to bounce back and realise that despite everything, I am a "thoughtful, talented and lovable" person that people like to work with.

Justin Paul, Founder and Principal Consultant, Brygstow Consulting

Bouncing Back is a refreshing take for anyone looking to boost or regain their prospects professionally. It supports you in seeking and seizing opportunities and is delivered in a style that is easily accessible. The High-Cs Transition model gives people great insight into the journey that we go through between having a setback and bouncing back!

Joe Holmes, Project Manager, Financial Services, iGO4 Limited

Bouncing Back delivers practical and positive advice to get you going in the right direction and I really enjoyed the affirmative tone of the book. As a full read from front cover to back, or as a reference to dip into when needed, this book is everything you will need in your modern career to survive and prosper. The Tool Kit in Chapter 15 is a real gem; read it and keep it in your back pocket – this book will help you to succeed.

Kevin Bennett, Manager, Centre for Workforce Excellence,
South West Institute of TAFE, Australia

I was thoroughly hooked by *Bouncing Back*. Having had a career that has bounced a couple of times, it was good to be reminded that our careers are in fact a journey – sometimes we hit a pothole and other times we may need a trampoline to help us back onto our path.

This book is that trampoline – I loved the real, practical advice that it offers and the exercises it asks you to do. *Bouncing Back* also reminds us that we need to be true to ourselves in order to be a survivor. It is a practical and immensely sensible route map to a sustained thriving career, and is full of top reminders for those of us who could bounce a bit higher!

Sarah Daniels, Chartered Practitioner,
The RedCat Partnership Limited (Health and Safety Consultants)

RICHARD MAUN

BOUNCING
BACK

How to get going again
after a career setback

mc Marshall Cavendish
Business

Published in 2012 by Marshall Cavendish Business
An imprint of Marshall Cavendish International

1 New Industrial Road, Singapore 536196
genrefsales@marshallcavendish.com
www.marshallcavendish.com/genref

Other Marshall Cavendish offices: Marshall Cavendish Corporation, 99 White Plains
Road, Tarrytown, NY 10591 • Marshall Cavendish International (Thailand) Co Ltd.
253 Asoke, 12th Flr, Sukhumvit 21 Road, Klongtoey Nua, Wattana, Bangkok 10110,
Thailand • Marshall Cavendish (Malaysia) Sdn Bhd, Times Subang, Lot 46, Subang
Hi-Tech Industrial Park, Batu Tiga, 40000 Shah Alam, Selangor Darul Ehsan, Malaysia

Marshall Cavendish is a trademark of Times Publishing Limited

A CIP record for this book is available from the British Library

ISBN 978 981 4382 10 6

Printed and bound in Great Britain by TJ International Limited, Padstow, Cornwall

For Julie in Canada, Kevin in Australia
and Julie in the Studio – for making it happen!

CONTENTS

Do you to need to recover from redundancy or dismissal, secure that promotion, rebuild your business or start over again? If you do, then welcome to *Bouncing Back*, the book that is here to help. Right now, we might not know exactly where we're heading yet and that's okay – this book is here to stimulate thinking and to provide us with practical tools and ways of approaching the world. We can decide what works for us and what will help us to make the most progress in our current situation. Please read through the detailed contents section that follows and ask yourself:

- Which items am I most interested in?
- Where do I need a helping hand?
- How can this book support me on my journey?

PREFACE

SECTION ONE
CONTEXT & QUICK STARTS

1. BOUNCING BACK FOR REAL – A true story

2. MODERN CAREERS – Welcome to now

3. THE GYROSCOPE – Increasing our self-esteem

4. THE ESSENCE OF SUCCESS – Three key rules

5. GETTING STARTED – Simple steps to take

SECTION TWO
SKILLS & INSIGHTS FOR LONG TERM SUCCESS

6. THE HIGH-Cs TRANSITION MODEL – Key stages on our journey

7. PHYSIS – A useful word nobody has heard of

8. DOING FEELINGS – Making friends with ourselves

9. BUYING TIME – Increasing horizons to reduce panic

10. THINKING ABC – Giving our brain a workout

11. WHAT'S THE OPPORTUNITY? – Seeing the market

12. SALES SECRETS – Method matters

13. EMBRACING SOCIAL MEDIA – Free, fun and useful

14. MAKE A CHANGE – Learn to keep learning

15. TOOL KIT – The essence of bouncing back   176

16. HELPFUL HABITS –

OTHER BOOKS BY RICHARD MAUN   212

ABOUT THE AUTHOR   218

Preface

Bouncing Back is here to support us when the world of work suddenly changes for the worse and we're left wondering what happened and what to do next. Perhaps we lost our job, or our business crashed, or the market place disappeared, or our organisation hit us hard in some way. We might have been partly to blame, or we might have been an innocent party, or a victim of someone else's greed or stupidity or callousness. However, what happened *has* happened and we have to deal with the disaster and then strike out in a new direction.

Bouncing Back is based on real-life experience, practical approaches and clear thinking. It's full of useful tips and tools, designed to get us thinking and acting positively, so that we can make progress. The stories all come from real people who have had their identities disguised, but they are real. I'm one of them. I've taught people how to cope with stress, how to think in useful ways and how to watch out for the behaviours that get in our way… and I've had to use my own teaching to help myself, which was both humbling and a good life lesson – because being resourceful is a key skill. Lots of teachers become distanced from what they teach because it doesn't affect them anymore, so it was a shock for me to get dumped back almost at the start again and have to line up my tools and assets and help myself to survive. And I have survived; I bounced back and have been happily surprised at how life has changed for the better. You'll find out more about my journey in the first chapter. The rest of the book is based on the lessons my colleagues and I have learnt and it reflects what we have had to discover, to embrace, to let go of and to have a go at in order to move forward.

OUR KEY DEVELOPMENTAL TASK

This book is about developing. Because when we experience a setback, it's all too easy to fall back into safe patterns of being – to draw in our horns and to get *stuck* thinking great thoughts, without being able to put them into practice. This is normal stress-related behaviour and to do it for a couple of days or weeks is perfectly understandable. Any longer though and we start to get too set in our ways and run the risk of becoming stuck in the quicksand of our miserable, unhelpful place. This would be a bad habit to lapse into and this book is here to enable us to develop *new and helpful habits.*

An example of a helpful habit might be to add one new contact to our social media sites each day, whereas an unhelpful habit is to rubbish the whole social media arena as a dark corner of the world where 'oddballs and crazy, lonely types' hang out.[1] Pause for a second and reflect: Which habit will keep us stuck and which one will enable us to make progress?

---

[1] The world is a rich mix of people and we can all find our way and our voice. And we need to retain a sensible perspective – you can choose and control what you say in social media circles and, therefore, who you invite into your space.

Keep this concept in your mind as you read the book and ask yourself:

- *What helpful habits do I need to develop?*

One new habit is highlighted at the end of each chapter for us to consider.

MODERN CAREERS – MODERN ATTITUDE

We need to understand that the 'traditional career', where we work loyally for one organisation for a long time and are rewarded with pay rises and promotions (for length of service and work done), is receding fast. Like the rainforest being gutted to feed an expanding population, the traditional career of service-and-reward has largely been replaced with what I term the *Modern Career*, where life is full of twists and turns as we move between 9-to-5 jobs, consultancy work, self employment and a portfolio lifestyle. The idea that we joined Old-Biz & Sons as a boot cleaner and diligently worked our way up to Office Manager over a 40-year period is now largely confined to the pages of a Dickens novel.

With the rise of social mobility, higher and further education, social media and relatively easy credit, the modern career is what we have to reconcile ourselves to – where we have to make things happen for ourselves, where we have to be resilient and where we have to keep learning. When we do these things our 'career' continues and we enjoy the next phase of the work part of our journey. By knowing the inherent truths about modern working life – that it's not a straight-line climb to the top, that it requires us to create our own opportunities and that we need to keep adapting and evolving – we realise that being able to bounce back is an essential skill to have, because we'll have to make several bounces between starting our first job and eventually retiring.

This book is here to support our journey and to remind us that we are good people who want to work hard and do a good job. Sometimes we need a gentle nudge to get through the problems before us and that's where *Bouncing Back* comes in – it's full of support and designed to be simple to read, easy to understand and powerful in its application. Reading the book gives you the chance to reflect and to take stock of what you have and which options you can create for yourself. Then you can take easy steps to create the next part of your Modern Career and enjoy a brighter future.

YOU CAN CHOOSE

While this book is full of things to encourage clear thinking and practical actions, what you *actually* decide to do about your situation is really up to you, because we alone are responsible for our actions and inactions. It's worth remembering that *not* doing something is still a decision, even if it's a decision for inaction. Staying still is a choice, just as getting up and walking around is. Sometimes not *doing* anything is actually the smart thing to do – taking time to reflect and work out more options could well be the best course to take. Of course, we also need to judge when it's time to make a move and get going.

Therefore, you can use this book to support you in the way, or ways, that work best for you and you can choose to agree or disagree with, think about or ignore the contents. My invitation to you is to do two things:

- Dip into it and explore the chapters that interest you.
- Trust your intuition to tell you where these places are.

If you want to read it from front to back then please go ahead, or if you want a pick-and-mix approach then your intuition will be able to guide you. You can choose what to do and how to do it. What you do and the consequences of your decisions rest firmly on *your* shoulders.

MY BACKGROUND

I'm a specialist in supporting people as they look for work, transition through an organisation, build and lead teams, make tactical and strategic decisions and come to terms with difficult and stressful times in their modern career. I work with people in organisations to enable them to understand themselves at a deeper level, to think more clearly and to communicate more effectively. This involves using coaching approaches, training and development sessions and consultancy support, depending on the needs of the person or the organisation. I also have an unshakeable belief that if you want it badly enough you can have it – the capacity for human resilience and progression is amazing. For my own part I've survived four redundancies, being bullied at work, running a loss-making business, dealing with product failures, setting up my business and re-training myself at the same time, the collapse of the economy and my client portfolio when the markets crashed in 2008/2009/2010, and the exhausting work of writing, editing and marketing five books. I know what it's like to be in tears, to be frightened that the house is going to have to be sold, to be so fed up at the latest nasty surprise that you can't be bothered to get out of bed and to wonder if your peers are secretly laughing at you, glad that *you* took the bullet and not them.

All of this is what has made me successful, because I haven't blindly turned up to work for 20 years and just 'got in with it' –

I've had to learn and re-learn and take calculated risks and think about what works and what doesn't. Experience and reflection are powerful tutors that have served me well.

I've survived all of these things, have thrived and have continued to enjoy my working life, develop new skills and shape my life so that opportunities are created and new horizons appear for exploration. I have *Bounced Back* – and you can too!

ACKNOWLEDGEMENTS

Without Martin Liu and his clear thinking this book wouldn't have been created and published, so he gets my first thank you for his brilliant support. Also the team at Marshall Cavendish all worked hard to turn the manuscript into a book, including Chris Newson and the unfailingly polite and helpful Janine Gamilla and their design, editing and production colleagues. So thank you for your care, attention and professionalism.

Some of the ideas around *physis* have been shaped and explored by my Transactional Analysis peer group, where we meet and discuss theories and approaches, so it's with great pleasure that I'd like to thank: Tim Davidson, Joe Holmes, Christine Hyde, Jenny Labbett, Paul Robinson and Gary Telfer. It's useful to get creative feedback regarding my ideas, so thank you team for sharing your views and thoughts.

There are some local heroes whom I'd like to thank, because they helped me to start networking again and to find my feet. Step up: Sarah Daniels (my great networking chum) and Julie Bishop (my wonderful radio co-host) and finally Sara Greenfield (my social media expert) – you're all fabulous, thank you. Sean Kent was the first Tweeter I met in real life and without early adopters like him, the social media place would be much duller, so thank you too, Sean.

My writing support team is always on hand to keep me focussed on completing the manuscript and to natter away the small hours when I'm in need of a diversion and have a new idea to test out on them. They're a great bunch of people who are generous with their support and kindness, so thank you to Steve Tracey, Frances Donnelly, Ria Varnom and Julie Holmes.

Finally, love and happy thank yous go to Lucy, Theodore, Oscar and Harvey, for interrupting me when I most needed it, for asking 'why' all the time and for making me laugh. And Beck gets the last and biggest thank you for being the power who creates the space to enable it all to happen. Thank you.

Richard Maun
Norfolk
England

Richard can be contacted via:

Modern Careers Blog:	www.richardmaun.com
Facebook Page:	Richard Maun – Modern Careers
LinkedIn:	Richard Maun
Twitter:	@RichardMaun
Skype:	richardmaun
Business:	www.primarypeople.co.uk

SECTION ONE

CONTEXT

&

QUICK STARTS

Bouncing Back For Real

– A true story –

PRACTICAL & GROUNDED

Bouncing Back is about surviving *and* thriving. It is full of practical tools, techniques and insights culled from the shared experiences of myself, my clients and my colleagues, and they have all been proven to make a difference. Bouncing back doesn't need to be complicated, expensive, take forever or require us to have some special aptitude for 'bouncing' – we all have the potential to succeed and we can all be resourceful and learn new things that help us.

We're starting this chapter with my own story, because I have used all the tools mentioned in this book and I've had to live and learn too. I like my story. I've worked hard, made mistakes and kept going through tough times. The same applies to the other people in the book and nobody (myself included) has had special privileges, easy shortcuts or a fairy godmother to wave a wand and magic us into a happy future. Your situation is unique and the exact nature of it will be different to everyone else's. That's fair enough. However, a good way to approach things is to accept that we can all bounce back; we just haven't done so *yet* – but we will arrive at a better place, we just don't know *exactly* when that is or what it will look like.

As you will see from the rest of the chapter, my business has bounced back and I created my own opportunities: I collected evidence and trusted my intuition to make sense of the facts and, above all, I kept going. Blind struggle is just pointless, but if we don't keep going in any direction then we really will struggle to get anywhere at all.

IN A NUTSHELL

My story is straightforward: I have survived redundancy and business downturn, but am now once again *thriving*. I have been managing my own training and coaching business for nearly 10 years with some success. Before that I had a 'traditional career' in operations management, which seemed to involve more than my fair share of redundancy and having to bounce back from that. Then in 2009 the banking crisis caused 80% of my client work to disappear as organisations struggled to sort themselves out. I couldn't sell my old courses because nobody wanted them and I went from being a busy consultant racing along at 100mph to a quiet consultant creaking along at 5mph, wondering what to do next. Then I noticed that not *all* my colleagues were quiet like me and I began to piece together a new business strategy, partially by noticing what was working for them and adapting it to suit my own business.

> Success is often based on taking note of what is already working well and by replicating it. We can borrow from others in order to make life easier for ourselves.

In essence, what I did to bounce back (from 2009 to the present) was to get my business accredited to the Institute of Leadership & Management so that I could sell formally *certificated* leadership and coaching courses... and... (deep breath)... I learnt how to sell and assess a brilliant personality profile called LaunchPad; phoned a friend and went networking with her to get me back into the habit; started a weekly blog full of career tips and useful learning points at www.richardmaun.com; repackaged my old training notes into new products and added a shop to my blog so I could sell them; asked a friend for free office space so I could write a business book; taught myself how to use Twitter and invested time in social media; secured my own radio show; developed Skype-coaching clients to enable me to work overseas without leaving my desk; started speaking at networking clubs and business conferences; made sure I kept networking; set up a simple sales spreadsheet and developed over 50 new sales opportunities for myself; won new locally-based clients; wrote two more business books; changed our home finances so we could buy time and keep going and learnt to enjoy making new friends and taking the children to school.

That, in a nutshell, is my story and some days I was elated with success and other days I couldn't be bothered to switch on my computer – I was *that* fed up. Life is never a straight line to the stars.

When I started over again in 2009 it felt like all I had was a blank sheet of paper and a deep sense of frustration that in the great game of snakes and ladders that is life, I had climbed up lots of helpful ladders only to step on a massive snake and slither all the way back to square one. At the time of writing this I love my new life and, like looking after a garden that needs constant attention, I'm still trying new things and experimenting in order to keep growing and developing.

A REAL EXPERIENCE

I'm not going to pretend that my journey was easy. Along the way there were happy days, frustrating days and then some black days when it felt like a pointless uphill struggle and I wanted to switch everything off. In fact that's what I did to begin with – I swept my desk clean, switched off my computer and had a week off, and then as that had been a great success, I took another week off. I gave myself permission to feel too sad to work and too angry to focus and after my little holiday I then gave myself permission to write a book about being a father. That led to a meeting with my publisher, who didn't want my dad book, but commissioned me to write *Job Hunting 3.0*, which then led to a contract to write *How To Keep Your Job* which in turn led to a contract for this book. At the same time I changed my business as I described above and made new friends and won new clients. I also began speaking at local networking events and conferences (as I always wanted to do more of that kind of work) and instead of grumbling that I couldn't sell training to old clients, I started to enjoy selling myself to new groups.

> My motto became:
> **Do more of what people want!**
> (Because you never know where it will lead.)

EVERYTHING LEADS TO SOMETHING

At one speaking event I was invited onto a local community radio show to talk about my latest book, so a few weeks later I went to the studio and had a happy hour chatting on air with the DJ. At the end of my piece I walked out of the studio and with one hand on the front door, about to exit and drive away, I had a small epiphany, and said to myself:

Richard, you've always wanted a radio show of your own and here you are about to walk out of a radio station. Don't waste the opportunity! Do something!

So I turned around and knocked on the door of the station manager's office, walked in, introduced myself and said:

'I hope this doesn't sound too silly, but I'd like to have my own show and I have no idea where to start. I'm happy to get a broom and start there. Can you help me?'

And he did. I worked out my own training schedule, practiced hard, invited a colleague to collaborate (as I realised two heads were better than one), wrote some sample shows, practiced a lot more, made a heap of mistakes, wrote a script for a business show, honed things with my colleague and made it plain that we didn't care what time of day or night we were broadcast, but that we weren't leaving without a slot. Our persistence paid off and we now broadcast our *Business Life* show each week on Future Radio[2]. And we both love it to bits.

I'm sharing this with you not to sound like some pretentious radio 'luvvie', but because I had mentioned my radio ambitions to a few colleagues before and yet was clueless how to realise it – and 18 months later I had made it happen by simply following my heart and being brave enough to ask for support.

The show is for a charity station so we don't get paid, but the rewards are more than just money and it's been a great lesson for me that whatever we do can reap huge rewards. We don't have to always charge for our time and can choose to give gifts to others. I love the work, so it's a 'job' that is a total pleasure to do. I have a fixed commitment each week which means I have had to

---

[2] Check out www.futureradio.co.uk and look at the schedule for show times. We broadcast live to the community and across the net to the world.

change my working patterns and as a result am now much more productive at the start of the week as I feel that I have to 'earn' the time to go and do radio. It's also enabled me to meet new people, laugh hard and long and has expanded my business horizons. And all that from literally changing direction and asking for what I wanted!

FACE THE UNCOMFORTABLE TRUTH

Back in 2009, I was busy. So busy that 'home' was just the place where I stopped occasionally to collect clean shirts and repack my briefcase for the next few days of work. And then it all ended. I had a really, *really* bad day:

'Yes, it's cancelled,' I was told, 'we can't place the students we've trained and so we can't take in any more to add to the stockpile. Organisations are shedding staff and struggling to survive, so they're not interested in expensive student-consultants for a year.'

And that was that... a prestigious, award-winning programme for middle and senior managers was switched off, along with a team of highly respected trainers, coaches, support staff and about 60% of my business. Just because something has run successfully for a long time doesn't mean it's immune from a market that has collapsed. It doesn't matter how good we are or how much we work out clever sales schemes to stay in the market – if there *is* no market we have to face the facts. *We're bust.*

My colleagues and I knew the end was in sight, but we had hoped we could put together a rescue package, change the course, buy time, move the debt-risk profile around, stand on one leg and squint – anything to stave off the final decision, but it was all to no avail and the course was closed. My work there as a lecturer and coach, bar some run-out contracts, was done and dusted.

And then it got worse.

Other clients stopped booking training work and then got rid of their training departments altogether as they flinched and gasped in the wake of the economic hurricane that blew through the developed world. Banks collapsed and long-established 'safe' businesses imploded as credit dried up and consumer confidence evaporated. For me it meant that training hadn't just slipped down the corporate agenda, it had been torn off the bottom and rammed through the shredder. Colleagues with similar businesses, who would previously have booked me to support them on their courses, stopped calling because they too didn't have any work, let alone need extra hands to help them.

To put this in simple terms: by the middle of 2009 I had lost 80% of my forward revenue and clients. Gone. Bang. Done. And there was nothing I could do about it.

20% did not make for a business. I wriggled and cursed and tried to deploy clever thinking, but it was no use. Life had changed and the business world had been altered forever. I had a choice – I could ignore it or I could square up to it and get going. I'm not ashamed to admit that I ignored it for a while and assumed that with a bit more creative thinking a handy solution could be found. But when all the options were exhausted there was just one thing left to do – acknowledge that my business really had died. The unthinkable had happened and the truth was I was going to have to start again. That was a shocking moment and yet a happy one too – the shock forced me to let go of the recent painful experiences and clear both my mind and desk to create room for the new. And that was when I really started to bounce back.

> We begin to bounce back when we embrace the uncomfortable
> truth and then create space to invite in the new.
>
> (Until that point, we're just playing at bouncing back.)

YOU ARE NOT ALONE

This is my story. Yours will be different, although perhaps similar in parts. The one thing we have in common is that we are not alone. Across the workspace in all corners of the country, we are two people amongst millions and although our grief and struggle is unique we also share it with all the other people in similar situations. We are not the first. We are not the last. We are together. And together we can find comfort and get on with our working life. Remember that.

I WAS LUCKY

I was lucky because my industry was leading the trend – along with web design and marketing, the training market was one of the first to get hit with the global downturn. This may not sound like luck, but it did mean that I had to face up to the new world there and then, unlike other colleagues in 'safe' industries such as local government who sympathised at the plight of engineering and manufacturing from the safety of their air-conditioned offices.

Getting hit first meant that I had to take stock and respond quickly and that by the time the other industries had followed suit, mine had stabilised and started to regroup. Not that you want to get hit at all, but sometimes when a group of bankers make a greedy hash of things that's what is going to happen.[3] And the truth is that we're all in it together: whether we elected politicians who did

[3] I realise that bankers aren't the only ones to blame, but they did manage to sell products that they didn't understand, to people who didn't understand them either, which has to be an ethically and morally bankrupt way to do business.

nothing, quietly took a million-dollar bonus without wondering where the money *wasn't* coming from, failed to pay taxes in good order, or leveraged purchases against unsustainable personal debt while ignoring the impact of compound interest rates. The majority of people did something to contribute to the downturn, however well-intentioned we might have been at the time.[4]

WHAT BIG CHANGE DID I MAKE?

It tends to be a truism that if we only make little changes then we only get little results. In terms of bouncing back, I knew that I was going to have to do some new and significant things to make a real difference – otherwise I was just 'rearranging the chairs', as a colleague likes to say. To paraphrase him, I needed to get some new chairs!

After I realised that the world had changed, nothing happened next because there was nothing to happen. A few smaller pieces of work needed to be completed and a few tiny projects were left for me to sort out, but in general nothing was happening because the market had frozen solid as organisations worked out what shape they were in and what shape they needed to be in to survive over the short term. Then gradually I started to marshal my thinking, focus my energy and do new things. My long list of activities earlier in the chapter took a couple of years to unfold, and if there was one big change that I made which spurred on lots of smaller successes, it was this: I made a conscious decision to use my time (which I had in abundance) to get connected to the world through this new thing called 'social media'. I asked myself two pivotal questions:

---

[4] As an example of collective culpability, the Italian government has been quoted in *The Week* as needing to make 25 billion Euro of budget cuts during 2012. In 2011, however, they failed to collect 120 billion Euro worth of taxes from the population. Who's kidding who here?

> **Question 1:** Who really knows I'm here?
> **Answer:** Nobody, really.
>
> **Question 2:** How many people know what I have to offer?
> **Answer:** Not enough.
>
> **Thought:** So what will I do to change that?
> **Answer:** *I will go and talk to people!*
>
> (It's really that easy if you make it so.)

I spent time increasing the number of LinkedIn contacts I had, joined discussion groups, widened my circle of friends on Facebook and plunged into the world of Twitter by following one friend and then, trusting her good taste, systematically following all her followers who lived locally. This gave me a kick-start and I've not looked back – when I started I had about 50 contacts in all and now I have around 4,000 across LinkedIn, Twitter and Facebook. I've made some great friends, found new clients and had support when I needed it – it's amazing how rich our social media life can be and that help is often a click away. We'll come back to social media in a later chapter, but for now here is what I always tell clients who are looking to bounce back:

> Social media is free.
> It's a route to market yourself.
> **A *free* route to market yourself!**
>
> How can you make this work for you?

WHAT DOES BOUNCING BACK REALLY MEAN?

We all set our own targets and we each have different ways of measuring our success. People might think that bouncing back is about simply replacing what we have lost in terms of money and status, and while that might be the case for you, for me I've learnt that as we can never go back into the past, bouncing back is about *creating a new world for ourselves* that makes us happy. This can include money for sure, and it also includes things that we were missing before – maybe time with our children, the fun of pursuing a leisure interest, time spent learning a new skill or investing in ourselves by exploring new horizons and venturing beyond our immediate comfort zone.

> ### BOUNCING BACK...
> ... is about creating a new world for ourselves that brings us enough satisfaction to feel that we have truly moved on from the past.
>
> We have survived and are once again thriving!

I have bounced back and have been surprised that my working world is so different from what it was before. I drive less miles, spend more time with my children, have more fun and generally am not so stressed out. I'm aware that I earn less money than I did before and I'm happy with that as I've knowingly traded earning time for fun time. Some of the key differences between my former busy life and my 'bounced back' life are:

THEN	NOW
• Drive 30,000 miles per year	• Drive 12,000 miles per year
• Working nationally	• Working more locally (and internationally thanks to Skype coaching)
• No time for children	
• Working week = work only	• More school runs and more playing
• Two books written	
• Earning a reasonable salary	• Working week includes fun (radio)
• More tired and less happy	• Five books written
	• Earning enough money
	• Less tired and more happy

From a career perspective I have carried on with my personal development, enjoyed the process of developing new products and been energised by the fun of finding and working with new clients. If there is one story that summarises my journey it is this: Last year I took the children to a large toyshop and we bought two remote control boats; a trawler and a harbour patrol boat. When the weather was warm in Spring I took the children to school and instead of a mad scramble to arrive on time we would leave the house early and sail the boats at the local boating lake. The sun was bright and cool and the sky a clear blue, and the boats skittered happily up and down the lake as the children made them zigzag and play chase. After a while the batteries ran down so we packed up and then went to school. What a way to start a day! We loved it!

For me, taking time to enjoy a simple pleasure in the sunshine was proof that I had moved on and really bounced back, because

I was happy with my working world. And I still am. So in reading this, maybe ask yourself:

• *What would you like to do differently?*

WORK LIFE IMBALANCE

The phrase *work-life balance* is often used although it is *meaningless* in practice, because we always have a natural imbalance of time taken between work, keeping house, raising a family, paying bills and finding time to play. I don't know anyone who works for exactly the same amount of time that they play, so why aim for a balance? A balance is also almost impossible to achieve (just try balancing on one leg for a while and you'll soon tire and fall over). What's better is to achieve something more relevant to our busy modern careers – a happy and fulfilling work-life *imbalance*. Aim to spend at least two hours a week on non-work related activities and enjoy yourself, knowing that this is still part of a working week as it energises us and gives perspective and depth to our lives. It doesn't matter what it is that you do, as long as it isn't work. If all you do is sit quietly and listen to some music, that's good enough.

SETTING GOALS

Goals are good, even if the only one we have is to 'have a happy life', because that allows us to ask questions such as: What does 'happy' mean? How much happiness do I need? When I started I created little goals, such as to make it through the next six months, to find 10 new contacts on social media sites, to go networking twice a week or to write one new training course. I didn't scare myself with unattainable targets and I deliberately kept my goals small, local and achievable. Have a look at the following prompts and start to think about a few goals for yourself:

- Work location
- Work content
- Work amount
- Work direction
- Home life
- Fun time
- Personal growth
- New skills
- New horizons
- Cherished ambitions

Think about your working life last week or last month and write down the key points in the table below. Then think about how the list might be different in two years' time. Take a pencil and write in things that make sense to you… don't edit them, just write them down.

Last week / Last month my working life contained these things:	In the future it could have these things in it:
1)	1)
2)	2)
3)	3)
4)	4)
5)	5)
6)	6)
7)	7)
8)	8)
9)	9)
10)	10)

WHAT HAVE I LEARNT?

This book is about learning and challenging ourselves to do things differently so that we achieve a new level of success. However, it's always valuable to reflect on our journey and to learn from others. In writing this book I've reflected on what I have learnt and here are the key lessons that I've taken from my experiences:

Richard's Learning Points:

- We need to choose to bounce back instead of choosing to stay stuck, because everything flows from this decision.
- Money isn't everything.
- When life hits a trough, taking time off is a smart move.
- Having fun makes for a more productive week.
- The more we talk to people about the reality of our situation the more help and support we receive.
- Meeting new people leads to new opportunities.
- Lots of opportunities create lots of interesting ways to bounce back.
- Big progress can require big changes.

You are welcome to take from this book what most fits your need at the current time. Whatever your current situation is – whether your job has disappeared, your host organisation has collapsed or your business has suffered a major setback, you can take heart: the place you are in now is *temporary*. It will not last forever. By taking action and finding ways to channel your energy, you too can happily bounce back.

SUMMARY & NEW HABIT #1

Summary

After reading this chapter please take time to reflect on what messages you have taken away and what thoughts it has sparked for you. Learning how to bounce back from tough times is a critical skill for a happy working life – although our stories will be different, we can all be resourceful, find energy, make new choices and get help so that we can continue our journey and arrive somewhere good. Our current situation is only temporary and every one of us has the skill and resources to bounce back – we can all survive *and* thrive.

OUR NEW HABIT TO HELP US BOUNCE BACK:

- Make sure we have some working time and some leisure time each week. The combination works in harmony to improve our thinking, creates new opportunities to meet interesting people and increases our confidence. Our aim is to achieve a happy work-life imbalance because that is easier to maintain.

Modern Careers

– Welcome to now –

TRADITIONAL VS MODERN

Now is the time of the *modern career*, a phrase I coined last year to describe today's working world and to differentiate it from the traditional career we may have thought we were going to have when we first left school. The notion of any kind of career might feel like a bit of a sad joke to us if we have suffered from an unfair decision at work, a bullying boss, a customer who reneged on their debts, a major investment that turned sour or the after-effects of a global downturn. What good is a 'career' when we're sitting at home wondering who is going to pay the mortgage for the next few years? What is the point of even aspiring to a career if the world says:

'Thanks for all your hard work, early starts, late finishes, weekend working and selfless dedication to our organisation – thanks for that, but you're *still* going. Bye!'

Organisations, businesses, market trends, interest rates… they all promise so much and yet have an unhealthy tendency to let us down.

In a fickle modern world the only things we can ever rely on entirely are ourselves and our ability to adapt to changing circumstances, and that is the essence of a modern career. The world is unstable, rapidly changing and advancing at a speed that would be inconceivable to our grandparents. If we take social media as an example, two years ago I had colleagues who were marketing themselves simply as 'social media experts' and now they're specialising and becoming 'Twitter experts' or 'Facebook experts' as each site becomes ever more complex.

AN ESSENTIAL PERMISSION

In order to have a fulfilling modern career, which is the practical heart of bouncing back, we need to accept a fundamental truth about our part in our success:

> The responsibility for our modern career
> is ours and ours alone.

We need to give ourselves space to accept our feelings and to accept that the world can be a complex, dangerous, stupid, unforgiving, vindictive place. And at the same time it's also full of happiness, opportunity, excitement and love. We have to allow ourselves the freedom to stop blaming the world for our misfortune and to accept responsibility for our modern career. Once we do this we become powerful, assertive people who are much more likely to succeed.

It is unfair when something awful happens, and we can feel all of our hurt and mistrust and *still* accept that we are responsible for leading ourselves out of the mess. Working life isn't going to come knocking on our door.

WHAT MAKES A MODERN CAREER?

If a 'traditional' career meant joining one company in the post room and working our way up to Managing Director over a 40-year period, before bowing out with a carriage clock and a sausage roll buffet, then a modern career is the antithesis of this. One of the defining elements of a traditional career was to be asked 'what do you want to do when you grow up?' This rather tedious question suggested that a) all possible careers were known to us and that b) having never worked before we would know exactly what we would like to do. Replying drily along the lines of:

'Well, I want to do something not yet invented called *business coaching*, using an approach to help people communicate effectively called *Transactional Analysis*, which I won't hear about until I'm 30.'

… would have been prescient bordering on genius, but in reality would have just sounded arrogant and earned me a disapproving look. Instead of knowing exactitudes and making silly guesses to appease well-meaning adults, we can know that a modern career is built from the following general guidelines:

---

7 TENETS OF A MODERN CAREER

1. Not knowing exactly where we will be by retirement.
2. Not knowing when retirement will be.
3. Being able to re-train if we need to.
4. Being able to work in a variety of ways, such as an employee, a consultant or in our own start-up business.
5. Being responsible for our own money management as pension rights are increasingly eroded, we have periods out of work or wish to self-finance a change of direction in life or work.

6. Having job-hunting skills. In my experience the UK's favourite sport isn't football or fishing – it's having an amateur hack at getting a job by *trusting to luck*.[5]

7. Knowing our own skills. We need to have a good sense of what we like to do, what we are good at and how we add value. These may emerge over time in response to experience.

Looking at this list above, it's likely that none of these things, or the reality that the world of work is a messy and unpredictable place, was taught to us in school. If a typical job tenure these days is between two to five years then we have considerable scope for changes over the span of a 40- or 50-year career. We can almost guarantee that we will have a period out of work; that our first work-related skill specialisation won't be our last and that whatever we know today won't be good enough in 10 years' time. A modern career has the advantages of flexibility, responsiveness and the opportunity to make changes, so there is freedom to explore and design a working life that works for us.

SKILLS FOR A SUCCESSFUL MODERN CAREER

Given the predictable *unpredictability* of a modern career, we need to get to grips with three basic skill groups and be proficient in them if we are to succeed. We need to understand what our strongest abilities are and where our developmental tasks lay. Our strongest abilities are the things that lead us forward and which we excel at – perhaps writing clear prose, or being great at meeting new people and building useful relationships. They don't necessarily have to relate to a special work-related skill. For example, I always thought that I was an average

---

[5] It's astonishing that the one skill essential to a successful working life – knowing how to get a job – isn't generally taught in schools. If you'd like to get ahead then check out the book *Job Hunting 3.0*, which I wrote to fill this knowledge gap that I have encountered so often in clients.

planner but a great presenter… so I decided to capitalise on the latter and find work that played to that strength. Our developmental tasks may be easy to describe and yet can take time to hone; for example how we work under stress, how we deal with conflict situations and how to approach risk-taking decisions. We're all a 'work-in-progress' and as long as we keep learning and developing in our modern career we will be well-placed to keep going.

The three skill groups that we need to think about are:

1. Specialist skills
2. External skills
3. Internal skills

MODERN CAREER SKILLS NO. 1 – SPECIALIST SKILLS

These are the direct work-related skills that we have been trained in. These skills are particular to our role or industry and can include:

1. **Technical language**
2. **Trade skills**
3. **Craft skills**
4. **Process skills** (such as computing, presenting or selling)

As we move between roles and industries these skills might deepen or they might be lost and replaced with new ones. Without specialist skills we will lack credibility in our role or industry and will struggle to add value. Therefore, we need to make sure that we fully understand what is required of us and make an effort to fill gaps and develop an appropriate level of competence.

- Which areas are we technically strong in?
- Which areas still require further development?

MODERN CAREER SKILLS NO. 2 – EXTERNAL SKILLS[6]

These skills are the ones that others can see us using. They
are part of our everyday working life and they fall into three
groups. When we examine what makes people successful in an
organisation we find that they excel at:

1. **Productivity** – being able to manage our time, work under
   pressure, plan and prioritise effectively and meet deadlines
   to the required quality standard.

2. **People Skills** – the way we interact with others and make
   friendships, resolve conflict, negotiate agreement, lead
   others and exert our influence.

3. **Public Relations** – the wider influence we have in our
   organisation and the myths and truths people believe
   about us. We need to be effective in getting our message
   out so that the senior managers know about us, like us and
   have a healthy respect for how we add value.

- What do others say about our external skills?
- Which one of the three groups do we need to pay more
  attention to?

MODERN CAREER SKILLS NO. 3 – INTERNAL SKILLS

These are the skills that we carry with us but are not visible.
We might infer their usage from close observation and can
measure them through psychometric profiles. They are
affected by the mood we're in and the way our physis[7] is
flowing. They are a mix of who we are and what permissions
we hold in our heads. The seven internal skills are:

---

[6] These three core skills form the basis of the book *How To Keep Your Job*, which looks at
them in detail and also includes the Organisational Impact Score concept to enable us to
remain objective about our true performance.

[7] See the later chapter on physis.

1. **Agility** – the way we cope with change, embrace new ideas and new ways of working and our willingness to let go of old things to create space for new ones.
2. **Determination** – our willingness to succeed. This isn't simply our 'energy'; it's the force of will that we deploy to ensure we reach our goals.
3. **Humility** – our ability to apologise, admit ignorance, be prepared to seek and take support, and whether we see others as equals or inferior to us.
4. **Learning** – how much and how readily we allow ourselves to take on board new skills and how much we reflect on problems and make sense of what worked and what didn't, for our future benefit.
5. **Reliability** – our level of consistency and whether others can rely on us to turn up to work, to deliver work on time and to be successfully delegated to.
6. **Resilience** – how we accept the world as it is and make changes to take us forward, and how we respond to knockbacks and find new purpose.
7. **Thinking** – our innate use of sensible processes to think through problems, resolve dilemmas, understand risk, check facts and be wary of assumptions.

- How would we score ourselves out of 10 for these? (1 is low, 10 is high)
- What is our greatest asset to help us over the long term?

Looking at these skills, where are you now? What is your least developed area that you would benefit from investing some time and energy in? When you go for a job interview which area is going to help you get the job and which one could derail your chances if you don't take positive steps to improve it? If we're going to be asked searching questions then the first one we can prepare ourselves for is:

What's the worst question I can be asked at my next sales/job/ acceptance interview?

If we know the answer, then we can identify which area needs to be developed, and if we don't have the time to make significant changes we can at least practice a reasonable answer to the question so that we don't make ourselves look foolish.

ONGOING TRAINING

When I was at school we would sit in long rows for exams, facing the raised stage where the teachers would sit like prison guards, alert and on the lookout for suspicious activity. I vividly remember a senior teacher addressing us as we prepared to sit the last paper of our final exam. He said with a reassuring smile:

'Well boys, this is the last exam you will ever have to take.'

I believed him and then spent the next few years cursing at his blatant untruth as exams were inevitably part of getting a degree, driving a car and learning technical work skills. In fact life seemed to be one long exam, so when I was invited to sit a particular coaching exam in later life I rebelled and declined – I'd enjoyed the learning, was extremely proficient at using the tools and processes and decided that I didn't need a piece of paper to show clients. I could get on well enough just by being good at my job… and I was right. Clearly we do need exams if we want to follow a particular career path, but the point here is that people sometimes mistake passing exams for learning.

If you're going to an interview and get asked if you 'like learning', you'll probably say 'yes of course'. However, how well could you answer the following questions?

- What have you learnt over the last three years?
- How have you developed?

Think about them for a moment. They are searching questions and ones that are hard to lie about if you simply 'like learning' but haven't actually done any. Notice too the part about 'three years' – the timescale is deliberately short so that under pressure we have to talk about recent events and can't rely on something we sweated through 15 years ago and may have now largely forgotten about.

An ability to learn is highly prized by future employers because if we are good learners they can teach us a new role. This means that our previous background matters less, and we become more employable. At an interview we need to able to demonstrate our ability to learn, through our stories that show how we have grown and developed.

SELF-CHECK ON LEARNING

QUESTION 1: What have I learnt over the last three years?	**QUESTION 2:** How have I developed?
My answer is:	My answer is:
Think about courses you have attended, books you have read, workshops you've created or mentoring that you have been part of. How have you learnt from mistakes? What would you do differently?	Think about positive changes other people have noticed in you, attitudes that have shifted and where you have become more thoughtful, flexible or responsive to change. What do you now do less of, or more of?

WHERE ARE WE GOING NEXT?

Because we want to bounce back we need to have something to aim for, even if we subsequently decide to change direction. Do we want to keep working in the same way for the same sort of organisation, or is it time for a change, even for a few months, until we feel ready to move on again?

The next step on our modern career might be to:

- Find another full time role
- Look for consultancy work
- Set up as a sole-trader offering products or services

- Buy-in to an existing company
- Work in partnership with a colleague

We don't necessarily have to continue the path we were on before. We can choose a different path for the time being and see where it leads us.

CASE STUDY – HANNAH

After working hard and achieving the success of being made a partner in a law firm, Hannah realised that she was fed up. She often worked an 80-hour week and was duty-bound to respond to her clients' needs, even if that meant working all weekend, so she decided to make a complete change. After spending a quiet weekend reflecting on what she was good at and what she enjoyed, she resigned and then re-trained as a life coach, moved houses to release some capital and started a new business. After working flat out for 15 years she realised that money and seniority were becoming a thin reward and she wanted the freedom to set her own working patterns and to do a job she loved, rather than one she had fallen into on the advice of her parents. She had always liked working with clients and had a reputation for being a friendly person who was easy to talk to, so she capitalised on that natural warmth and swapped legal skills for coaching skills.

IDENTITY ISSUES

Making a change, whether we are forced to or by choice, creates stresses and fears as we confront doubts about the future and question our decisions. This is perfectly normal and a good sign – if we're not at least a little anxious we could be sleepwalking into danger. Part of our concern will often be the underlying issues we have about our *identity*: namely how we gain recognition among our family friends and peers and what we say about ourselves when asked about our job at social gatherings. Our job title, the level of responsibility we hold, the number of staff in our team, the size and elegance of our desk, car or office all help to inform people about us. They suggest importance, prestige, attainment, social standing and intellectual ability. We don't exist in the world as simply 'Richard' or 'Julie', we become 'Richard the coach' or 'Julie the managing director' and our job title and all it stands for becomes part of our identity and our sense of well-being. We feel comfortable because 'we know who we are'.

When we lose our job or our business is closed, we are stripped of all that in an instant. We arrive at work at 8.30am as a successful manager or technician with a job title and responsibility and exactly 31 minutes later at 9.01am we leave as a 'civilian' with just our name and an empty briefcase. This is traumatic and can leave us feeling bewildered and deeply saddened. What will we tell people at the football club? If we do the school run will other parents stare at us? How will we introduce ourselves at social events? How do we feel about telling people that we used to be a manager but are now a job seeker? It's a humbling experience and one that can really destabilise us for a while as we adjust.

Our identity is central to our sense of well-being and it's extremely uncomfortable when we have to deal with a seismic shift in that. However, part of our developmental task when bouncing back is to embrace new ways of being and to come to terms with our new identity. We can change the way we introduce ourselves to other people and remember that losing our job doesn't mean that we have suddenly become bereft of all our career skills.

For example, instead of saying 'I used to be a senior receptionist' we can say 'I'm a fully-trained hotel receptionist looking for my next role'. The former is very passive and backward-looking, whereas the latter is more assertive and forward-looking. Or instead of introducing ourselves as 'an out-of-work director' we can say that 'I'm an experienced sales director setting up a consultancy business'.

If you read any of the examples in this chapter and instinctively thought 'Oh no, I could never do that', stop and think about why you had that thought. In my experience of working with people who are fed up and in the process of bouncing back, it's often because there is something about the role or title that we're uncomfortable with. Perhaps we know some interim people and don't think they do a great job, or we wrongly assume it's an option for people who can't hold down long-term employment? Nobody likes to own up to a prejudice, but if we are dismissive then there's nothing wrong in at least admitting to ourselves that something is amiss and checking the facts. All styles of employment have value and we don't want to let silly stereotyping get in the way of our options. Life is difficult enough without us limiting our choices and making it harder for ourselves.

When I started my own business I felt a bit foolish because I wasn't comfortable introducing myself as the Principal of Primary People. That just sounded odd, even though it was perfectly correct. However, it was just like the initial stiffness of a new pair of shoes and the more I met people and introduced myself the easier it became, until the business incorporated and became a Limited Company, promoting me into the role of Managing Director. My business card changed, as did my identity, and again it took a while for me to feel comfortable with that title. I was muttering one day about 'not really being a proper MD' when a friend overheard me and, laughing, made the following observation:

'Is a "proper" MD someone who is hired to run an already-established organisation, or someone who sets up his own business from scratch and develops and sells his own products?'

'Well both are, of course,' I answered without hesitation and then paused and laughed. Of course it's true, we can be an MD of any size of organisation and it's a title we can be proud of – if we're proud of the work that has gone into getting us there.

BECOMING AT EASE WITH OUR IDENTITY

As our world changes and we respond to the transitional process of bouncing back, we can make a conscious effort to reappraise our sense of identity and become more at ease with ourselves. If we tell new stories that have a positive outlook, we can begin to adapt to our new selves.

IDENTITY & STORIES

Our sense of identity will shift in response to our changing situation and it's okay to feel sad for what we have lost and, at the same time, to think about our skills and talents. In taking a practical step to forge a new identity we can easily establish ourselves as a sole-trader, a consultant or a freelance specialist while we transition. We don't have to be devoid of an identity – we can create something that suits us. Identity is also intertwined with our stories and we can learn to craft these so that our sense of self remains intact. For example:

- Our job was made redundant, not us as people.
- We can proactively make the difficult decision to close our business, instead of watching it slide away from us.
- We can choose to set up our own business, instead of telling people we've been thrown on the scrap heap.

What do you say about yourself now? How can you update the story so that you present a positive, measured, assertive, proactive face to the world? This will provide us with a sensible feedback loop as a positive story will reinforce a positive sense of identity.

The mantra here is very simple – *when we're okay about telling our story, then other people will be okay listening to it.*

I now have a range of identities to choose from and have found that it's fun to mix and match them to suit the occasion. As well as being a managing director, I'm a university lecturer, a business coach, a published author and now a radio business-show host. There's no reason to stop at one identity and we can have fun creating ones that we feel comfortable with. It's our life and it's our modern career.

SUMMARY & NEW HABIT #2

Summary

Traditional careers are largely a thing of the past – we're now in the phase of the modern career, where we have a pick-and-mix world of job opportunities, role changes and new directions to travel in. Over the course of our working life we can easily have a wide range of jobs and move between several areas of technical specialisation. We can create our own opportunities and if we keep our skills polished and keep on learning then we are well-placed to have a successful modern career.

OUR NEW HABIT HELP US BOUNCE BACK:

- Keep an open mind. We might feel overwhelmed by the choices before us and the fear that our next job almost certainly won't be our last. However, if we keep an open mind and consider each option on its merit we will create useful career-enhancing opportunities for ourselves.

The Gyroscope

– Increasing our self-esteem –

OUCH! THAT HURT!

When our career takes a tumble and our job disappears, or our business goes bust, our boss bullies us into an early exit, or the world flips upside down for a moment and throws us out, we are often *hurt* – bruised and confused. We might pretend that we're fine and soldier on, but inside we will tend to feel a bit battered and maybe hard done-by. With a world full of vacuous celebrity 'wannabes', wealthy pop stars, jet-setting bankers, devious politicians and faceless technocrats all enjoying a first-class champagne lifestyle, we tend to compare ourselves unfavourably and feel that we have slid to the bottom of the heap.

If someone punches us we often cry out – 'Ouch! That hurt!' But when that someone is a manager who treats us badly, they are protected by their organisation and beyond our reach and even though we still shout out, nobody hears us. We complain, but the organisation stares back at us implacably, hidden behind a smooth wall of jargon that seeks to depersonalise our situation.

When all this happens we have taken a knock: to our feelings, to our pride and to our sense of worth. This can all feel very de-stabilising. We will explore feelings later on in the book, but this chapter is about thinking of what lies at our core – beyond thought and beneath feeling, we have *self-esteem*. We need to understand that this inner part of ourselves is there and that our task is to become resilient by taking care of it and knowing that whatever has been thrown at us, we remain a decent, lovable, talented and worthwhile human being.

THE INNER GYROSCOPE

Our self-esteem gives us an inner balance – it's like an eternal gyroscope, spinning round to keep ourselves upright. However, when we get a knock the gyroscope is jostled and for a time it spins erratically as it struggles to regain its poise and restore order to our self-esteem. In the process our identity shifts and wobbles as we wonder who we are right now and what might become of us. We might feel a great sense of loss and we might experience a nagging doubt that we are not whole in some way and are lacking a key component. In the upheaval something has become detached from us and while our gyroscope struggles to right itself we feel out of step with the world around us.

This is perfectly normal and is something that I've seen in many clients from a variety of backgrounds all the way up to senior director level. Often people assume that the big boss will be fine with the world because they have contacts to guide them and a huge payoff to cushion them. Often though, the truth is that they can fall from a high place into a deep chasm.

> **OUR SENSE OF SELF-ESTEEM**
>
> ... is about being confident, talented and thoughtful.
> We belong in the world and have a right to a decent life.
> We are as good as the next person and although we may
> have had difference experiences in life other people are not
> better than us, or vice versa. It is our right to work and this
> is not diminished by our age, sex, race, colour, creed, religion
> or family situation. We are important because we count as
> talented, lovable human beings. We can learn to be resilient
> and can make new choices for ourselves.
>
> (Keep repeating this until you've really accepted it.)

CASE STUDY – BOB

I remember working with a managing director whose factory had been shut in a corporate reshuffle, leaving him jobless. When I met him he had not had any interviews for over a year and was quietly despairing that in his mid-50s his working life was over. When we talked he also disclosed that he simply couldn't see how he could work again – he wasn't young, he had grey hair, he lacked a degree, he didn't have any significant management qualifications – from his viewpoint he really had nothing to offer. Internally his sense of self-esteem had been battered and he really felt that his situation was hopeless. Simply teaching him how to write a CV or how to conduct himself at an interview wasn't going to make enough of a difference to him. It would be window-dressing, when what he needed was a deeper level of support to get his gyroscope fixed and regain his sense of self-esteem.

We worked together and explored the unfairness of his

situation and the heartache of not having had a single response to his job searches for over twelve months. We also started to list all the skills and talents that he *did* have and he began to realise that for 10 solid years he had been an effective leader, managed his business effectively and had sold products and led improvement teams. His factory hadn't been closed for being a failure – it had been relocated to ensure its success continued, albeit with a cheaper labour force. We talked some more and then Bob listened to me telling him about his life and in doing so he began to regain his sense of self-esteem. He heard about his successes, the facts that showed what an effective leader he had been and the stories that demonstrated his abilities. His gyroscope was settling down and in doing so he let out a tiny little smile, like a secret thought escaping. I asked him what had just happened, but he just smiled broadly this time and said that he felt ready to go job hunting – he was putting things in perspective and becoming resilient.

CASE STUDY – SUSAN

Susan had worked as an administrator for local government and then paused to have a family. When her sons were at high school she decided that she wanted a part time job, but found it hard to find the motivation to be successful. Her previous role had been over 15 years ago and she knew that now that she was older, less qualified and unable to compete with the young graduates flooding the market, her chances were limited. At least, that's what she kept telling herself. Her self-esteem had hit rock bottom and she openly said that:

'I have no worth. I don't count.'

She was so used to seeing herself as a wife and mother that her only recognition had come from how well she cooked, sorted out the children's clothes or kept the house tidy. Although she hadn't suffered a single shattering setback such as redundancy, she had slipped away from the working world over the years and now needed to bounce back just as much as Bob did in the first case study.

In order to begin to bounce back she had to realise that she was entitled to a job as much as anyone else was and that she did possess useful work skills – she was an effective administrator and this had in fact continued in her volunteer charity work and school governor role. Faced with the facts, she realised that she hadn't entirely stopped working for 15 years; she had merely swapped some of the tasks about. They weren't paid tasks, that was true, but they still required diligence and skill to be carried out to a good standard.

Gradually, Susan realised that her skills had been there all the time, that she had relevant work experience and that her age was no issue to successfully holding down a job. After some coaxing she wrote a super CV and realised that she actually did have a lot to offer. Her little inner gyroscope began to sort itself out and over time her self-esteem rose to the point where she was able to secure two interviews, one of which led to a job as an administrator of a museum. Susan had learnt to be resilient and her self-esteem had increased – she just needed to get back in touch with herself and realise, like Bob did, that we retain our skills and talents in spite of setbacks. We just have to know they're there and celebrate them.

BUILDING RESILIENCE TO INCREASE SELF-ESTEEM

If we increase our resilience then our self-esteem tends to increase at the same time. This is because the external world weighs on us and creates fear and doubt in our minds. Our resilience is the force that meets this and holds it in check. As our resilience grows and pushes back these boundaries, our self-esteem flourishes in the space that it has created.

To build resilience we need to know that our doubts are just that – doubts. They are not facts. They might be there to protect us from making a mistake, but if they are getting in the way of us bouncing back we need to examine the reality by thinking about these questions:

SELF-ESTEEM STARTS HERE	
1) What skills have we retained? 1. 2. 3. 4. 5.	2) What qualities do we have? 1. 2. 3. 4. 5.
3) What else makes us employable? 1. 2. 3. 4. 5.	4) What compliments have we received? 1. 2. 3. 4. 5.
5) What is it about us that makes us a decent individual? 1. 2. 3. 4. 5.	

These questions are designed to replace doubts with a more *objective assessment* – when we answer these questions and look at the lists we can see for ourselves how good we are. If we read our lists out loud then the words travel into our ears and we will hear them. They are real. They exist.

Resilience comes from knowing how the world works and that our gyroscope might get jostled but it *never stops* – it's there at all times, spinning itself back into an upright position. If something nasty happens we can deal with it, face up to it and know that we still retain our inner goodness and our inbuilt strengths and abilities.

In addition, once we've read this book and learnt about transition, feelings, marshalling our energy and developing a useful appreciation of our place in the market, then we will have really grown and developed.

• How is your self-esteem now?

SUMMARY & NEW HABIT #3

Summary

When we experience a setback our resilience might dip, allowing our self-esteem to dissipate. This is perfectly normal behaviour and most people experience this at some point in their life, however confident they may appear to be. We can increase our resilience by reminding ourselves of the skills and talents that we continue to have – they didn't all fall out of our ear when we took a knock: they're still there waiting for us to acknowledge them. We are good enough to get a job or to start a business and we have a right to work. We're all good people – we can hang onto that.

OUR NEW HABIT HELP US BOUNCE BACK:

- Be objective about our situation and use appropriate language. For example, if we say 'I can't do anything' that is literally not true – we can all do something. Instead we can say 'I can do this and with support I could do that as well'.

The Essence of Success

– Three key rules –

LIFE CAN BE SIMPLE

Simple is powerful and simple is useful. Living in our current situation is tough enough and we don't need additional and unnecessary complexity cluttering things up. So if we have just enough capacity today to think about the essence of success then we can read this chapter, put the book down and then reflect on what we can do next. We can return to the book and dip into it, or read it from front to back as suits our need. The choice is ours.

THREE RULES FOR SUCCESS

If you're wondering how to bounce back successfully, or are currently stuck in the process of doing so and are wondering what to do – whether you're looking for work, striving to build your business or making personal changes in your life – then here are three simple rules for success:

RULE 1

Create your own opportunities

RULE 2

Trust your intuition

RULE 3

Keep going

---

1) CREATING OUR OWN OPPORTUNITIES

Sadly many people just get on with things and assume that they'll know what to do. I've worked with many good people who have grumbled that they can't find any work, and yet they have had no training or read any books, or spoken with any professionals (pub mates and coffee friends don't count). We can create our own opportunities by getting help, talking to new people, sharing a problem, networking widely, starting in a new direction and/or signing up for a training course.

2) TRUSTING OUR INTUITION

We can know what we want to do and can make good decisions if we learn to trust our intuition. We can ask friends and colleagues to help us generate options and can trust our judgement to choose the one(s) that we feel will work the best. We will discuss thinking in more detail later in the book – using our intuition doesn't mean that we don't think or that we take a blind guess. We might need to assemble some facts first in order to see a clear picture of the situation and then allow our intuition to guide us. The confident thoughts and feelings that we have inside us, just on the edge of our awareness, combine to steer us towards a choice that works for us.

3) KEEP GOING

It takes time to become successful and when we think of progress we're often stuck in the sticky mess of 'today' and would ideally like a quick fix. However, it can be smarter to think about where we would like to be in *two years' time* and to make sure we take care of ourselves in the long run. We can achieve life-changing things in two years – if we acknowledge that it can take time to make significant steps and that we have to keep going in order to achieve them.

YOUR 4TH RULE

If you added a fourth rule for yourself, what would it be? Take a moment to think about the phrases and sayings that have meaning to you and then write down a favourite one here:

MY 4TH RULE IS:

_____

_____

_____

SUMMARY & NEW HABIT #4

Summary

Three simple rules for us to follow are: create our own opportunities, trust our intuition and keep going. And we can add a fourth (and a fifth) of our own. We can write them all down and place them where we will see them every day – on the fridge door, in our diary, on the wall by our computer or in our wallet maybe. Then we will stand a better a chance of following them!

OUR NEW HABIT TO HELP US BOUNCE BACK:

- Keep our favourite rules in sight, so that we can be reminded of simple secrets to help us make progress. Write them on a piece of paper and stick them up somewhere that we will see them on a regular basis.

Getting Started

– Simple steps to take –

GETTING STARTED

What's the first thing you do when you are going on holiday? Do you pack, sort out an itinerary or buy suntan lotion and baggy beach shorts? It's none of those things because in reality the first thing we do is have a thought – that we'd like to take a break. Then we might talk to someone and share ideas, or go online and browse hotels and places that interest us.

The actual packing comes much later, after we have walked through a whole sequence of feelings, thoughts and actions. Bouncing back is the same and in my experience people are easily scared at the prospect of actually doing something. They have been dealt a shock – often a massive one – by their recent experience and are vulnerable, bruised and exposed. This is unpleasant and perfectly normal and often leads to inactivity. Our task is to recognise what the first easy steps are so that we can do something constructive, rather than sitting idly and waiting for the world to come to us.

CASE STUDY – BARCELONA 1992

I vividly remember being parked on the sofa during the Barcelona Olympics in 1992. My job had been made redundant and I was determined to enjoy the whole sporting fortnight from the comfort of the living room. I knew that in reality I was hollow inside, worried about how to get a job and struggling at the thought of writing a CV (easy-ish), driving to an interview (bit more nerve-wracking) and then meeting a total stranger and being asked personal questions about my life and career (absolutely terrifying). Given that the interview process was frightening for me, watching the Olympics seemed like a much safer bet for two weeks – I told myself I could do the hard bits afterwards. I was right too, although I didn't win any favours from my girlfriend or our housemate. I only got going when I realised that if I only had four weeks' worth of money left in savings I couldn't wait a month to begin looking for a job – having no job was bearable for a short while, but having no job and no money wasn't.

IT'S OKAY TO BE SCARED

It really is. Anyone in the process of bouncing back who isn't a little fearful for the future and the unknown is either lying to us (or themselves) or has a secret trust-fund that they haven't mentioned. Being scared is a natural reaction – but we can be scared and we can make a start. If we wait until we're entirely happy before making a start, then we might still be on the sofa when the next Olympics comes around.

STAYING SAFE

When we talk about 'safe' here we mean making things secure, painless and/or less risky. In my story I allowed myself to think of the scary bit at the end of the process and, of course, I increased my own fears in doing so. Had I broken down my thoughts into manageable little steps I could have progressed from one to another much more easily and I would have felt less anxious in the process. There's a well-known management phrase:

> ### Don't Eat The Whole Elephant...
>
> ... Or you might choke.
> Cut it into tiny portions for a safer
> and more digestible meal.

Staying safe is about keeping options in proportion and breaking tasks down into micro-stages, because sometimes that is all we can cope with. A friend told me about a famous pop musician who had a smash hit first album and plenty of chart success and then couldn't cope with the pressure of writing a second album. The problem was that the first time round the star was just being himself and could not have known how successful his band were going to be. But as he now had to guarantee success to please the record company, he tried to work out what the magic formula had been, which can be an overwhelming task. To make progress the band's bass player would visit him and say 'let's just write one word today' and he would literally write one word and then collapse exhausted. After a few months the series of one-words became ideas, then rhymes, then songs and later a second album. The pop star had bounced back and, together with his band, went on to even greater success.

TOP TIPS FOR GETTING STARTED

Here are some tips that I regularly share with clients. My invitation to you is to choose just **one** thing that you *can* do which you *will* do. Don't cheat and choose something you can do but don't want to, as that's just being a bit sneaky. Which one do you choose?

✓ **Stop doing things.** It can sound counterproductive to start by stopping, but we often have crowded lives and we need desk space, diary space and head space. What can you stop doing, or at least pause, to give you free space to grow in?

✓ **Get up.** It's easy to let a daily routine fall apart without a natural work focus or routine to pull our day into shape. But we can build our own day and that starts with getting up and out of bed at a reasonable time. For me, having to get up to do the school run forced me to get on with my day.

✓ **Spring clean.** We accumulate clutter and it crowds our house and clouds our thinking, because it encourages us to hold on to useless things that we can't quite find a use for *yet*. Spend time getting your house, office or desk in order. We can tidy up our physical world and throw things away, which is cathartic, and start the next day in a fresh clean space.

✓ **Buy a notebook.** I have found that getting a new notebook serves as a symbolic first step, because the act of purchasing it gives people tangible evidence of progress made. I would suggest a paper book too, as it's often easier to think and write, rather than to think while staring at a computer screen and trying not to play a game or surf the internet. (We will talk more about thinking later in the book.)

✓ **Make a list of key supporters.** I'm a big fan of sharing the workload, and attempting to do all the thinking work ourselves is setting a needlessly high bar to jump over. Who

are the clear-thinking, experienced people who can support
you on your journey?

✓ **Telephone each supporter and book lunch with them.**
Using the telephone is an active action, whereas simply
emailing others can be passive because we have to wait for
them to respond... if they actually get round to it. We want
to get into the habit of being active, talking to people and
getting out of the house. Lunch, or a mid-morning coffee-
and-cake meeting means we have to go somewhere and it
gives us a purpose for our week. Whenever I get stuck, I
make a list, line up my cake-friendly supporters and go and
talk to them. I've never failed to collect new leads, options
and ideas in the process.

✓ **Do something you really want to.** In order to get going and
find our energy we don't necessarily have to do more 'work'.
We can award ourselves with a holiday and invest energy
into something that we want to do. For example, before I
started my business I took two months off and wrote my
first book – I decided that since I had a gap between work
I could fill it with a long cherished project. In 2009 when
work dried up I realised that July and August were going to
be deathly quiet, so rather than get frustrated, I swept my
desk clean and wrote half a book about how to be a great
dad. It was great fun and helped me to get rid of some of my
anger at watching my business implode.[8]

✓ **Do something new.** If we do the same old things we get the
same old results. After my book writing fun I realised that
nobody in business knew I existed – my client base had
disappeared and I needed to find some new people to talk
to. I decided to join a new website that was making waves –

---

[8] Nothing is ever wasted. My half a book was enough to get a meeting with my publisher,
whom I hadn't seen for two years. At that meeting the book *Job Hunting 3.0* was born and
my writing career took off again.

Twitter. It was fun and I've found new clients and made new friends and the fact that I had a growing network of contacts also helped to secure my next publishing deal. Learning about tweets and Twitter-folk was much more fun than sitting home alone feeling angry that the world was collapsing and when I started I had no idea how useful it was going to be.

✓ **Volunteer.** While the above tips are more directly work-related, here I refer to a local project that you might be interested in. A friend of mine started to bounce back by volunteering for a local landscape conservation society, and he went out felling trees, digging ditches and maintaining safe pathways. Volunteering brings us into contact with more people; we can network with our colleagues and at the same time feel that we are using our time productively. At interviews, candidates are increasingly being asked how they filled their time while looking for work and by volunteering they have a good story to tell. What interests you? What would you like to volunteer for?

✓ **Pay for professional support.** I included this option because it's the one we often overlook, on the assumption that we're not feeling that bad – we can tough it out and stoically carry on regardless. We probably can, but at what cost to our family, who have to take the brunt of our anger and frustration? I've had a business mentor and helpful therapy sessions and they were both valuable experiences – the chance to talk and be heard was incredibly restorative and I wondered why I hadn't done it before. If we have a sore back we'd go to a physiotherapist, so what's wrong with seeing a psychotherapist or similar? If it helps, do it and if you've never had it – try it.

SOCIAL MEDIA IS SOCIABLE

I know, I mentioned the dreaded T-word earlier. Many of my colleagues fall into one of two neat piles – those who think Twitter is a rich seam of life, to be enjoyed and explored and played with, and those who think that those in the first group have a) got way too much time on their hands or b) are wasting their time anyway. People are entitled to their opinions, of course, however it can be foolish to dismiss social media platforms out of hand as that could limit our choices.

We will come back to social media later in the book, but for now we need to remember that not engaging with social media can be a grave mistake in a world full of busy people who tend to carry smartphones. Do you use email? Well, technology futurists are already predicting its demise, because SMS and Twitter are faster, require less infrastructure and often get dealt with more promptly. If you love social media then I'm preaching to the converted and I'm sure we will be tweeting shortly (I'm @RichardMaun). If you currently despise social media – and you're entitled to your opinion – then just start to think that you *do* want to *bounce back* and anything that can support this has got to be worth serious consideration.

Social media is genuinely sociable and when we engage with it we 'leave' our house and go out into the wider world and talk to people. Despite the sceptics and naysayers social media can be used safely – we just need to follow the rules and apply common sense to what we do and how we do it.

TAKE SIMPLE SAFE STEPS

People often talk about 'making the leap' but personally I can't think of anything I'd rather do less in a difficult situation than make a leap into space with all the elements of danger and uncertainty. Corporate CEOs sometimes talk about building a 'burning platform', which is great if you have a corporate bank account to finance the construction of a new platform once you've burnt down the old one. Of course, nobody really wants to be a big cheese on a burning platform and inadvertently turn themself into a sticky business fondue.

What is more effective though is to build a bridge from here-to-there rather than trying to leap over the gap. Often the people who take small, easy steps are the ones who make the best progress. An easy step from a developmental perspective can include:

- ❖ **Finding the facts.** What don't we know about that we should?
- ❖ **Being pleasantly ignorant.** I like this because I've found that acknowledging our lack of knowledge or expertise in a good-natured way gives us permission to ask for help and to really ask all those 'silly' questions. An example would be getting legal advice. We might find it intimidating to be in a solicitor's office but it's quite alright to say 'I've never done this before – what is the process, what is the timescale, what is the budget and what do I need to be asking you?' Experts often forget that their clients don't know what to ask for.
- ❖ **Taking stock of equipment.** Going to a sales meeting in a rumpled old suit isn't going to help our confidence much, so perhaps it would help to get rid of the creases, or buy a smart new suit and give our shoes a polish. If we need a new business card then we can take the time to have a batch printed up, so that we have something to hand over to people when networking.
- ❖ **Practice.** I used to get really nervous when going to interviews as I would fret about being late, not finding a parking space and so on. To get around this I would always

make a reconnaissance trip the day before and practice getting to the interview on time. That meant I could concentrate on rehearsing my interview questions and answers and not turn up in a sweaty heap, having rushed through town or taken a wrong turn.

We can take simple steps and we can stay safe as we do so. It's essential to keep the concept of safe steps in our mind because if not we run the risk of lapsing back into a state of nervous inactivity and that isn't going to help us. Safe is good – safe leads to progress.

SUMMARY & NEW HABIT #5

Summary

Making a start is important – we can choose to be active and make an effort to get ourselves moving again. The aim is to take small, easy steps rather than remaining inactive and suddenly having to make up ground with a huge scary leap. Even if all we do is to tidy our desk and go for lunch, we are setting ourselves up for success. Bouncing back is about many things, as you will find in this book, and at a base level it is about activity. It's not about sofa surfing!

OUR NEW HABIT TO HELP US BOUNCE BACK:

- Notice when we are inactive and consider what might be causing it. We can then decide to be proactive and take an easy step forward, so that we keep making steady progress to bounce back.

SECTION TWO

SKILLS & INSIGHTS
FOR LONG TERM SUCCESS

The High-Cs Transition Model
– Key stages on our journey –

THE JOURNEY

Bouncing back is about forward momentum and not simply about bouncing up and down in one spot. In order to successfully bounce back we need to embark on our own personal journey. When people are on a journey that mixes bereavement with development (mourning for what we have lost and celebrating what we have found) they tend to move through similar stages. This is comforting to know because it means that we can map the road ahead and give ourselves way-points to navigate along. How long we spend in each stage is up to us and we can revisit them until we're satisfied that we have what we need to make progress. This process of moving along a developmental route is described below by the High-Cs Transition model.

THE HIGH-Cs TRANSITION MODEL

This maps the stages we move through as we make the transition from problem to performance, come to terms with our starting point and create the next leg of our modern career journey. We tend to move through the stages in order, although some people race ahead and collapse back to an earlier stage if the initial euphoria of progress is tempered with a temporary setback. The seven stages are:

1. Stressful Chaos
2. Tense Calm
3. Free Cleansing
4. Anxious Consideration
5. Hopeful Catching
6. Careful Coordination
7. Joyful Celebration

1) STRESSFUL CHAOS

This is the first stage, when the 'storm' is happening: We are bobbing about in our 'boat', open to the whims of the wind, storm-lashed and unable to see land. The word 'stressful' might be an understatement – we're not sleeping, we're drinking too much coffee and we have an internal knot of panic that grips us constantly. Our time horizon is reduced to tomorrow, or to simply hanging on until we reach the weekend. When we're in this stage we can know that we will survive and that our little boat is *unsinkable*. We will survive the storm however rough the seas get. We don't yet know how exactly, but that doesn't matter. We will survive – all storms must pass.

Perhaps this is the time when our biggest client is disappearing, as happened to me in the first chapter. Or maybe we are being bullied at work, as happened to me before that, or our organisation is moving on and leaving us behind, or we were shown the door for some reason (almost certainly unfairly). And yes, I've experienced these too. But I'm not some kind of employment albatross who brings doom with him when he starts work; I'm just someone who has taken a few years to find a job that I excel in. I'm also aware that because average job tenures are between 2 and 5 years, if we've been in work for 20 years, as I have, it's highly likely that we will have bounced between jobs and egregious bosses[9].

- **Our developmental task for the Stressful Chaos stage**
  is simply to take care of ourselves and to allow others to
  support us. We can talk to people and get advice, have our
  voice heard and begin to form a sense of our options and
  the potential consequences.

2) TENSE CALM

This is the second stage, when we are becalmed. After the storm passes there is nothing, just an empty waiting while we look around us and gasp that we're still here. The bulk of the crushing stress has suddenly evaporated and we've stopped shaking. Something has changed. Maybe we had that particularly difficult conversation, or resigned, or left the organisation, or woke up and realised that business had changed, or that when we went to withdraw our weekly stack of cash there was nothing left in our bank account. Tense Calm involves those first days after the bad things have finally happened and we 'relax' because we know where we are now. We

---

[9] Egregious means massively incompetent; obviously and unquestioningly so. A word reserved for really 'special' people, who might just be in the wrong job entirely.

could be bust, jobless or facing a major restructure and, even though it's a miserable place to be in, at least we know we're here. A client of mine, Sarah, had always worked hard but received little support from her line manager who felt threatened by her and wanted her to leave. He made her life hard for a few months and then one day she was called in to a meeting and given an offer to 'resign'. She accepted the offer and when she told me about it she was smiling broadly, because although she was nervous about 'tomorrow' she knew where she was today and could stop agonising over her boss, her job and whether to make a decision. Tense Calm is about giving ourselves permission to pause for a few days and recover our energy. Maybe take a short break, or go out with some friends, or take time to read a book. The storm has passed and we can exhale at last.

- **Our developmental task for the Tense Calm stage** is to pause and acknowledge where we are. The important decision has been taken, perhaps to leave the organisation or to change careers or to start our own business. We may still need to attend meetings or discuss severance details, but the stress associated with them is greatly reduced now that we've taken the first move towards a better life.

3) FREE CLEANSING

This is the third stage, when we make a few basic changes. Once we have acknowledged where we are and that our career has stalled it's tempting to panic and rush off in the first direction that we can think of, or jump at the first opportunity dangled before us.

This is risky because the chances are fairly high that we will act in haste and make an unthinking decision simply to right a wrong. When people do this they often find that they've taken a wrong turn and have missed the chance to properly assess the situation. Spending time in the Free Cleansing stage helps us to make simple adjustments to start putting the past behind us and begin using up our store of frustrated energy.

The stage is called 'Free' because we're free to do something. Our power to act is returned to us and we need to wield it gently. During the storm in stage one, we'll have collected and stored all sorts of feelings because it's probably not safe to let them out. If we did we might find we've just punched our line manager or rammed the company car into a tree, and neither of these actions solves anything, however satisfying the initial thoughts might be. These feelings create stored energy inside us that needs to be released, like carefully allowing the fizz to escape from a champagne bottle to avoid blinding ourselves when the cork fires out.

In addition to releasing pent-up energy it's healthy to get our house in order and make some changes. By changing things around us we are *modelling positive behaviour* – these smaller changes signal the greater changes that are to come. Taking action reminds us that we are in control here, and even though we can't control the external world, we can re-establish our authority over a messy desk or a cluttered garden. We can be proactive and self-starting in a gentle and manageable way.

This stage is also called 'Cleansing' because in changing things we can let go of unhelpful baggage that is holding us back. In my case I had to come to terms with the fact that my customers were not going to simply put their training needs on ice and then defrost them in six months. I clung on to that hope for a few weeks

---

[10] Heaving a big sigh is often good evidence that we have let go of something inside us.

and then realised with a sigh that things had changed.[10] I had to let go of my false hope and cleanse my thinking. It was both painful and freeing at the same time.

If we never let go of things we don't grow, because we invest precious energy into maintaining the status quo. Let go and free yourself to make progress, or cling on to a now-defunct position and stay stuck. *Which do you choose?*

TOP TIP

Talking is Powerful

Talking to others enables us to bring to the surface our feelings and worries, our frustrations and our hurt. Spend time with people whom you trust and share your story with them. They don't have to offer advice or anything in return – just being listened to is a powerful and helpful way to cleanse our souls and to remind ourselves that we are worthwhile valuable people.

To move out of the Free Cleansing stage we can update our thinking and accept what is before us. We can also change our environment at a gentle pace and allow ourselves time to come to terms with our life now. If we want to do something we can take a look around our house, car, study or kitchen. What is one thing that we can add, move, tidy up or throw away?

- **Our developmental task for the Free Cleansing stage** is to recognise that changes in our physical world help us to make changes in our emotional space inside.

4) ANXIOUS CONSIDERATION

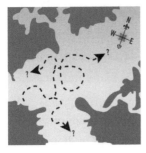 This is the fourth stage, in which we have to collect facts and draft our plans. In practice this stage causes anxiety because there are consequences to our possible actions and having just survived the initial aftermath from one grisly experience we do not want to blunder into an equally awful situation. A level of anxiety will sharpen our thinking and really make us check our facts. For example, a colleague was recently trying to decide how to spend his severance package and realised he could afford to buy a large chunk of land and develop a tourist business. When we talked it through and he realised the cost of converting, maintaining and marketing it and added in the fact that it was being *sold* (because the current owner couldn't make it profitable) he realised that although it might still be a good business proposition he needed to proceed with caution. People generally sell things for two reasons:

1. Either they are making healthy profit and want to realise the value of the capital assets, or

2. Their enterprise is uneconomic and they wish to offload it to a willing 'business expert' who loftily thinks he can do much better.

Both of these reasons are grounds for caution. In the former we might not be as good as the current owner and therefore struggle, and in the second the current owner might be right – he's happily taking our money and giving us a headache in return.

Anxiety makes us pause and take time to consider opportunities and to properly assess them. Consideration also means asking people for a fact-based commentary and getting a sensible appreciation of the risks. Simply asking people for opinions can make decision-making hard, as we have a tendency to ignore them anyway. Gathering information based on facts or experience is much more useful as we can test it against our plans and ideas.

- **Our developmental task for the Anxious Consideration stage** is to be methodical and trust our intuition. If an opportunity looks good and the detail supports it but something makes us nervous, then we should look again – we may have overlooked a potential pitfall.

5) HOPEFUL CATCHING

This is the fifth stage, when we get going. When disaster strikes, the effects can stay with us for months or years. Our feelings of loss, hurt and rejection can linger like the stubborn glow of a winter log that smoulders on for hours, even though the flames have gone out. This is okay and our feelings can take time to play out as we go through the process of bouncing back. This stage is called Hopeful Catching because we hoist our sails and hope the wind is there for us.

A friend said to me one day: *'You can't change the wind, you can only set your sails.'* This really made sense and helped to guide me. It gave me permission to accept the world order and to stop grumbling about it. We can only set our sails to catch the prevailing wind and, given the anxious consideration we have previously worked through, hope that we will sail on in roughly the right direction. In my case it meant noticing that not all of my colleagues had suffered such a dramatic downturn as I had. When I looked closely I realised that in a smaller market people wanted certificated courses as a way of justifying reduced expenditure. In order to catch the wind I reorganised my business and developed new certificated products that several new clients bought from me... the wind was blowing and I had to catch it.

This stage is about recognising that problems and opportunities exist at the same time. If we say 'I can't do anything because of the recession' then we give away our power to act. Instead we need to say: 'It's a tough environment and having given it anxious consideration I think this is the sensible step to take next.' When we say this and choose an easy action to complete we are hoisting our sails to catch the wind. We might need to adjust our rigging and tighten a rope, but even the lightest breeze can gently propel a yacht forward.

- **Our developmental task for the Hopeful Catching stage** is to recognise that we can't change the world but we can shift our perspective and take practical steps for action. We can spot trends and adjust our direction of travel to take advantage of them.

6) CAREFUL COORDINATION

This is the sixth stage, when we make progress and keep our eyes open for potential setbacks. If we imagine ourselves on a ship, sailing along, we need to make sure to note our speed and direction, that we steer clear of rocks and use the stars at night to get an accurate fix on our position. We need to have a feedback loop to check our progress and account for new information. Careful progress means continuing to take easy steps that are safe and risk-free, such as not placing all our money into one 'sure fire' business venture. Coordination implies that we have to consider those around us and how we interact with them, as well as make sure we have the right resources at the right quantity at the right time.

If our progress seems painfully slow we may need to pause here and go back a stage or two to see what is causing the problem. It's possible that we haven't really properly sorted out our feelings about a job, or perhaps a decision that felt right at the time now feels like it was the wrong thing to do. If this is the case then it's okay to strike our sails, drop anchor and regroup. I had to do this in the process of getting my business accredited to an external awarding body. I was slogging along writing procedures and trying to make sense of the forms I had to fill in and found myself making painfully slow process, caught in the trap of doing the right thing in the wrong way. So I stopped. Literally – I stopped doing the work and paid someone to do it for me. My assistant knew her way around the system and achieved in two months what I had failed at over six.

- **Our developmental task for the Careful Coordination stage** is to keep checking the speed and direction of our progress against our original plan. Are we going too fast, too slow, being sidetracked by irrelevances or making steady progress? What do we need to accept and change? If we keep asking questions and listen to the answers we can bounce back in a safe and orderly fashion.

7) JOYFUL CELEBRATION

This is the seventh and final stage, when we reach a sustainable place and can reward ourselves. We are still in our modern career and have reached a plateau in terms of this current transition process. How long this sustainability will last for is unknown to us, but we can be sure that it won't be forever and that we will have to start a new transition in the future. This is the nature of working life, although people often go through future transitions at a faster pace because they are more comfortable with the process the second time around.

At this time we are likely to be enjoying the feelings of success from surviving a tough ordeal. It's okay to keep one eye open for dark clouds on the horizon and we can reflect on the journey so far. We can find a way to say thank you to ourselves for persevering and to repay the kindness and support offered to us by family, friends and colleagues. The purpose of a reward is to recognise our hard work and also to enable us to draw a line under the previous experience and lay to rest any lingering 'ghosts'. We have already bounced back by the time we get to the this stage, but it's important to have an exit point to the process and to reflect on how we have developed.

As we turn around and look behind us at the distance travelled we can ask ourselves five questions:

5 REFLECTIVE QUESTIONS
1. What have I learnt?
2. How I have grown?
3. What did I do really well?
4. What is my reward for bouncing back?
5. What would I do differently next time?

Asking questions provokes our thinking so that we can extract life lessons and cement in new learning. This is the point when we can reward ourselves and enjoy our achievements, whether they are work, life or leisure based.

- **Our developmental task for the Joyful Celebration stage** is to choose at least one thing we have learnt or achieved, acknowledge it and find a way to celebrate that success. One deep change can cause ripples throughout our life that last for years and bring even greater success.

HOW TRANSITION WORKS

It's easy to read about the stages, allocate a week to each one and then confidently expect to be back in a happy place within a couple of months. However life is never that easy and depending on our depth of feeling, our resilience and our speed of recovery we can flip-flop between stages for many months.

If we get a knock we might catapult right back to *Stressful Chaos* and feel like we have to start the process all over again. In practice though people often make a mini bounce back because they already have a CV they can use, or they're more experienced at setting up a business and can do it differently the second time around.

People can also get a bit stuck at the *Anxious Consideration* stage and either rush about without sensible purpose or seem like they're doing all the right things, but are in fact hiding from some lurking fear. It's okay to be scared and it's okay to talk to people about it. Sadly people often don't do that though and instead make a good show of things without really addressing what's going on inside them. Transition is easy to write about but can be harder to live through – it's okay for us to find our own pace, to be angry and to take easy steps between each stage. Instead of unblocking the path by trying to shove the biggest tree out of our way, we need to look for the smallest twig and start there. After a while, we will have removed all the twigs and might be able to go around the big tree or realise that it's now easier to lift once stripped of its branches and surrounding debris.

SPOTTING INACTIVITY

Inactivity is about remaining in the same place. We might give a good impression of working hard and make lots of industrious huffing and puffing noises, but without making any actual progress. People can be scared of the unknown and as such stick with what they know, or they might genuinely not know what to do and flail around in the hope that if they produce enough activity *something* good will result. Here are classic telltale signs that we are stuck and need to stop what we're doing and make new decisions:

- We find ourselves repeating patterns of behaviour in the hope that *this time* we will get a good result.
- We talk a great deal without doing anything.
- We resist practical suggestions from colleagues by peppering our answers with 'but'. For example: 'I could do that, but I don't have the time.'
- We get angry with people so they back off and leave us alone, thereby avoiding having to explain ourselves or trying new things.
- We find ourselves delaying the important work until tomorrow.
- We spend time on distractions such as polishing our desk, excessive fact-finding or giving ourselves a preparatory task that must first be completed. If we're checking our emails, sorting our desk and chatting on Twitter when we promised to write our CV that morning, something is getting in the way and we need to face it and sort it out. Time spent chatting is healthy, but too much means we're stuck.

SUMMARY & NEW HABIT #6

Summary

Each of us goes through a process of transition when faced with significant change. We may find ourselves tossed about on the unpredictable seas of misfortune and uncertainty but we can know that all storms must pass and that the dark clouds will be replaced by bright sunshine and a lively breeze. Transition is part of life and moving through each of the seven stages is perfectly normal. How much time we spend in each stage is a product of our circumstances and motivation and we can work effectively (and use this book) to move smoothly through them. We can also ask questions to keep track of our progress, such as: Where are we now? Where do other people think we are?

The High-Cs Model of Transition is:
1) Stressful Chaos
2) Tense Calm
3) Free Cleansing
4) Anxious Consideration
5) Hopeful Catching
6) Careful Coordination
7) Joyful Celebration

OUR NEW HABIT TO HELP US BOUNCE BACK:
- Know where we are and what we're doing to progress toward the next stage. We need to be aware of our progress and to make sure that we're taking positive steps to a brighter future.

Physis

– A useful word nobody has heard of –

SMALL WORD, BIG IMPACT

- What is it that drives a person to work late into the night?
- What is it that keeps us going when we want to stop?
- What is it that enables us to survive and thrive?
- What is it that has spurred us on to read this book?

The 'it' in question is *physis* (often pronounced 'foo-sis'), which means growth. In all probability it's a word that hardly anyone has heard of, apart from botanists and Greek scholars. (The word *physics* comes from the word *physis*.) Homer (the Greek writer, circa 9th Century BC) used it to mean the intrinsic growth of a plant, and in his writings about Transactional Analysis, Eric Berne (1910–1970) used it to mean 'force of life', drawing inspiration from Heraclitus, who spoke about physis as the growth and change that comes from a person's inner spirit. The poet, author, naturalist and philosopher Henry David Thoreau (1817–1862) referred to it as coming from darkness into light; biologically, clinically and cognitively. In medical circles the word physis denotes growth and is a suffix to a variety of scholarly terms. And in nature it's the force that ensures a tiny seed germinates and then forces its way up through a concrete paving slab.[11]

In our terms, *physis* is the force that keeps us moving forward and continuing to develop. It's the wellspring of energy and power that we all have inside us. It's part of what makes us 'us' and how we use our physis to our advantage is what makes us unique.

THE PHYSIS GAP[12]

For me, the concept of physis unlocks potential and possibility. We don't have to accept what is before us – we can strive for new things, realise our potential and be happy and industrious in the way that we want to be. We are shaped and sculpted by the world around us – our parental influences, our physical environment and the rules and social graces that we live by. Sometimes these constrain us and sometimes they provide us with freedom to act. However, at heart we are all '*our own person*' and have made decisions about how we will live our life. Physis is the life force that acts on these incoming streams of information and bends and shapes them inside us, often outside of our awareness. The *Physis Gap* is the space where the external world ends and physis comes into play to tweak the stimuli before it enters our subconscious – it's the space where we filter and bend the world. Knowing about the gap is empowering because it gives us permission to consciously work with the world rather than simply having to accept it.

---

[11] Physis references: Books – *Eric Berne* by Ian Stewart and *The Dictionary of TA* by Tony Tilney. For the rest – Wikipedia and Google. And support from my TA colleagues, as mentioned in the Preface.

[12] This and what follows are my own developments on the concept of physis and I coined the term 'physis gap' about 7 years ago during a Transactional Analysis training session. Physis is an immensely useful concept that is seldom discussed and rarely researched, so for me this chapter is a key part of what makes this book so valuable.

THE TELEVISION TWINS

Here is a practical demonstration of the physis gap in action. I am fortunate enough to have identical twin sons, who are *monozygotic*, in that they were formed when one fertilised egg split and grew into two embryos. Oscar and Harvey are genetically identical, and are known as mirror twins – which means their hair whorls rotate in opposite directions, one is left-handed and the other is right-handed and they have both have one foot slightly larger than the other, one on the left and one on the right. However they are raised in the same house in the same way, although they are dressed differently and have their own identities. When they were 18 months old they were sitting facing the television and I was behind them watching over them. When they started to inch forward to touch the screen (a favourite game at the time) I said to them: 'Please do not touch the television.'

They both heard the same message in the same intonation at the same time. Harvey immediately sat down and remained motionless, while Oscar carried on forward and raised his hand, paused for a moment's reflection and then placed it on the television *stand*. They had both complied with the command, and each had done so in their own way, even though they are genetically identical. For me that is a powerful demonstration of the fact that we are 'ourselves' and the concept of physis can be used to reflect that.

SO WHAT?

We are going to bounce back. We are going to move through the High-Cs transition model, and take active steps to arrive at a new point in our modern career. However, doing this is going to require energy and we need to keep motivated – it's our physis that is going to enable us to do this. It's the force that keeps us slogging when all we want to do is hide under our duvet. It's the force that spurred you to buy this book and read it. It's the force that enables us to do energy-sapping things such as pay a mortgage, hold down a job, raise children and grow old at the same time. That's quite a remarkably complex and diverse set of tasks for which we have had little to no training. Our physis is the life force that keeps us growing and developing and we therefore need to celebrate it and engage it effectively so that we get to where we need to go.

ACCESSING PHYSIS

If physis is an unlimited force inside us that we can't create or destroy, then what can we do with it? What can we do to help ourselves? The answer is that we can encourage our physis to *flow*. To assist us let's consider a metaphor of a plant pot. Imagine that the pot and the seed buried inside the soil represents us and our potential for growth. As the seed germinates and pushes upwards, we grow. The seed will eventually sprout shoots and climb into the sunlight and keep growing, tall and strong, to produce a single healthy sunflower. We can't see the physis or make it do things, but what we can do is allow it to flourish. For example, if we put a ceramic tile over the top of the pot and block out most of the light, the seed will still germinate and grow, but it will take longer to edge round the tile or to push through a crack in it. Conversely, if we water the soil and add nutrients the seed may grow more quickly and could produce a taller sunflower.

Our job is to create the conditions for physis to flow. If this all feels a little odd then here's an alternative metaphor: Imagine that we are stone-built mill with a water wheel waiting in the mill race (the little 'river' that leads to the wheel). There might be water there, but not enough to turn the wheel... what we need to do is increase the flow of water by opening the sluice gates. The water then powers the wheel, turning the grindstones that mill flour from corn – when this happens we have used the flow of the water to good effect and in terms of bouncing back, we make progress.

It's up to us to water the soil or feed the seed, or open the sluice gates and grow. Here's how:

1. **Accept that we have an unlimited supply of physis.** It's never going to run out, so we can experiment and release as much as we like because it can only help us.

2. **Accept that we are thoughtful, talented, lovable people.** I've brought several clients to a standstill with these words as they pause for second and realise that they remain good people, even while struggling with a bad situation. They might be out of work, be persecuted by an uncaring organisation or be struggling to rescue their business from disaster, but that's all about the physical world. All of these things will pass. What remains unchanged is that we are all good people and that even if our world is chaotic or unhappy, our own skills and talents are not diminished. As you read this you can know that you are thoughtful, talented and lovable. You may not know exactly what your talent is *yet* but you do have skills and aptitudes.

3. **Accept that other people are often misguided or ill-informed, and can be safely ignored.** When I left a particular organisation I had an 'exit interview' with the Human Resources Director. He was polite and efficient and exuded all the warmth of a broken three-bar electric fire. As part of his checklist he asked me what I would really like to do in my career, to which I replied:

'Well Oliver, I'd really like to work as a consultant. I think that would be interesting.'

As I said the words I thought about the consultants we had had in the business and how they asked me the kind of questions I asked other people, how they seemed to enjoy a variety of work as I did and how they created options and solutions, like I could. I looked up and noticed Oliver looking uncomfortable.

'What's the matter?' I asked politely, 'did I say something wrong?'

He shifted in his chair, struggled to find the words and then calmly replied:

'The thing is Richard, to be a consultant you need to be... well how can I put this, er... um, you need to have plenty of *mental* horse power.'

'That's ok,' I said breezily, 'I have plenty.' I'd never even heard the term before. He shook his head.

'No Richard, you don't. You have some, but not enough and I wouldn't advise you go down that route.'

I was speechless for a moment. I couldn't decide whether to burst out laughing at his pompous attitude, accept it or challenge him. I chose the latter.

'Well thanks for that Oliver,' I said, 'but you're wrong. I'm smart enough, thanks.'

The point of the vignette is that people often make sweeping judgements or snap decisions based on whether they like us, rather than the evidence. We don't have to accept their commentary – we are in charge here and we will decide what works for us. As a gauge, would you tell a child he or she was too stupid to go into business? No, of course you wouldn't and it's the same when we're adults. We can ignore those who seek to diminish us. They might be well-intentioned, but we don't need that kind of support.

4. **Stop feeling like a fraud and feel fabulous instead.** The world isn't going to tap us on the shoulder and say, 'Ok the game is up, you can relax now that we know your little secret.' Many people I've worked with have limped along, afraid they will be 'found out' somehow. They compare themselves to stellar performers, decide they're not as good and that they shouldn't be in that profession at all. This kind of secret fear can cause immense stress and on the outside we might look full of composure and be working hard, but inside we're frightened to death that it's all going to come crashing down. If people have this fear it's because they're frightened of recognising that they are actually good at their role. They're great at what they do and can't quite believe that they can be this good, so they fret that it's a fake and a fraud. If you have these fears then sit back and give yourself permission to enjoy being talented.

5. **Check the facts.** People often make decisions based on feelings and confirm these decisions with a cursory glance at the details. Feelings are great and using our intuition makes sense, but if we ignore the facts we could be in for trouble. If we want to start up our own business we can do that very easily by calling ourselves a sole-trader – we don't have to have a business plan or impressive website, smart workplace or a degree in business. We can acquire all of these if necessary, but we don't need them to get started. However, it might pay to find out how many similar businesses there are in the area, and what people are currently paying for. We can ask ourselves:

What have we been assuming? Where do we need to check the facts? What have we not been doing that we can now do?

6. **Go into the future and take a look around.** This might seem a bit fanciful, but from a developmental point of view it can help to mentally experience the future, so that we get a taste of what's in store for us. When we do this we make an emotional connection with it and will work harder to get there… which waters the soil for our sunflower to grow. We can go into the future by taking three steps:

❖ **Step 1 – Move.** We can step into the physical space we want to be in in the future. For example, we can go and sit in the spare room that could be an office, visit a place where we want to work, or go to an art gallery where we want to exhibit. Sometimes we don't physically have to go to the new place, we can create a 'version' of the place – perhaps by changing chairs and our posture, or by standing up and surveying the imaginary scene so that we can bring it to mind.

❖ **Step 2 – Question.** Once we're in our special place we can ask future-focussed questions to take our thinking from the present into the future. We can ask ourselves: What do we see here? What activity are we engaged in right now? Who else is in this space with us? How happy are we to be here? What does it feel like to be here? What were some of the steps that brought us here?

❖ **Step 3 – Experience.** We can let the questions roll around inside our head and let our imagination drift as we search for answers and enjoy the moment. We can close our eyes, breathe deeply, conjure up images in our head and use our hands to explore our self-created virtual world. Experience is powerful and creates new decisions deep within us, awakens ambition and enables us to make decisions – even if we don't know how to complete the journey, we can find a way to get started.

7. **Allow ourselves to be flexible in the face of knock-backs.** In the process of bouncing back we may have tough days, delays to our plan, pitfalls and unforeseen issues to deal with. When these things happen we can pause and take a break – the world hasn't ended and we need to trust our intuition to find an answer and *re-plan the re-plan of the re-plan*. While it is galling to suffer a setback, it just means that our aim might have been a bit off centre – there is a job out there for everyone; we just don't know exactly where ours is yet. I've seen lots of people keep going when it gets tough and become successful in their endeavours. Our physis is there to support and energise us. If we don't have the answer now, then we might well have it after a good sleep or after a long walk.

8. **Review all of the above and change our self-talk.** If we say to ourselves 'I'm rubbish and I'll never get a job' then it's a fair chance that we will live down to these expectations. However, if we say 'I can find a job and I need some training and support to get me there' then we will likely go and find that support. I have a client who grumbled that she couldn't find work and had spent 18 months without success, so I asked her what training she had had in job-hunting skills and she said 'none'. We chatted for an hour to see what might be of help to her. Then I shared some stories of people who had been in a similar situation and who had changed their outlook. At the end of our time her self-talk had shifted from 'I can't do this' to 'I can find out how to do this', which is a radically different stance.

> **TOP TIP**
> **Think About Your Self-Talk**
> What do you really say to yourself?
> Who could you talk to, to begin making a shift?
> What positive words can you include in your new self-talk?
>
> As you shift your self-talk from negative to positive
> you open the sluice gate in your subconscious...
> the water rushes along the mill race and slowly the
> heavy water wheel begins to turn.

AFFIRMATIONS

Now that we have a list of practical ways to increase the flow of physis we can use *affirmations* to cement in our constructive self-talk and remind ourselves that we're only human and are not expected to suddenly become a superhero. An affirmation is a true statement that enables us to develop. Each one that we accept adds nutrients to the soil for our sunflower to grow. Personally, I'd take them all. You can't over-feed a seed in this model... read through the list and trust your intuition to guide you. Tick or circle the ones that have value to you:

- I can make a start without knowing the whole path (because I can keep myself safe)
- I can learn new skills and be good at them
- I can follow my heart and do what makes me happy
- I can change my life to suit my needs
- I can make mistakes and learn from them
- I can ask people for help with tasks
- I can think and feel at the same time

- I can pause and reflect
- I can find a way that works for me
- I can share my dreams and enlist supporters
- I can love myself and take care of my needs
- I can have ambitions and can take steps to achieve them
- I can know that my physis and my intuition are there to support and guide me
- I can take time to think
- I can go gently on myself
- I can know that I'm full of potential
- I can take pride in each step taken on my journey
- I can know that sometimes the smallest steps have the biggest impact
- I can enjoy my success
- I can rest on the way
- I can stop or change direction
- I can be active and get support when needed
- I am me
- I can live my life
- I _____ (write your own)
- I _____ (write your own)

Which ones caught your attention as you read that list? Write them on a piece of paper and keep them where they will be seen as you pass by. Affirmations enable our physis to flow because they open the sluice gates inside us to increase the flow of positive energy.

CASE STUDY – KIRSTY
Kirsty is a talented change agent whom I coached after her previous role had been made redundant and she was looking for

her next career move. She talked confidently and yet failed to go to job interviews and was generally very lacklustre about her performance until, acting on my intuition, I asked her if she felt like a fraud. The external confidence and the lack of activity didn't add up and something was amiss. She looked at me, burst into tears and then revealed that she felt like she didn't belong because she didn't have a first degree.

She had been worried that people would find out and think less of her. I put her previous achievements into context and she could see, for the first time, that she really did have substantial skill and that her work had nothing to do with her academic attainment. She had been asked the question she most dreaded and – to her surprise – nothing bad had happened, and she was met with only good comments and positive affirmations about her talent. This experience enabled her to let go of her fears and as a result the flow of her physis dramatically increased. So much so, that she was able to convince the CEO of a major multinational to listen to her pitch for a new method of managing complex projects. Kirsty is now a successful consultant and continues to impress people and invent her own modern career.

THE PHYSIS FLOW METER

The important thing about physis is that it continues to flow, because the volume per se is of no use if it's static, bottled up or constrained. The tips and hints in this chapter are all concerned with flow because we all have physis in abundance – our task is to release it so that it flows and powers our onward development. If it was a twisting, bubbling river we could dip a flow meter into the middle of it and take readings to check that things were okay. Where physis is concerned though we can only go with our instincts and score ourselves in terms of how well we're doing right now. Have a look at the physis flow meter below and score yourself for where you are this week… remember that if you're still in a miserable job or working hard to keep going in the face of hardship, it might be that your physis is actually flowing at high speed in order to get you out of bed each day and turning up at work. Draw the needle where you feel you are now and then in the box underneath write in one thing that you will do to increase (or maintain) the flow of physis:

THE PHYSIS FLOW METER

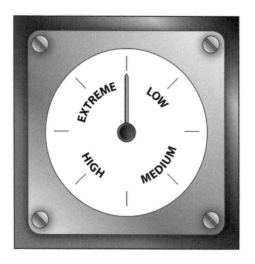

In order to maintain or increase the flow of physis I am going to:

_____

_____

We can return to the flow meter in a couple of weeks and see how we are feeling then and compare scores with how we currently feel. Physis is the wellspring of energy that powers us forward and if we keep an eye on our personal flow meter we can ensure that we're topping up on affirmations and taking care of ourselves so that we give our little seed room to grow.

SUMMARY & NEW HABIT #7

Summary

When bouncing back, physis could turn out to be the most useful word that we've never heard about. Knowing that we have this life force inside us is comforting, because we understand that we do have the power to keep going and to work our way through the transition from disaster to future success.

OUR NEW HABIT TO HELP US BOUNCE BACK:

- Keep a sharp eye on our personal physis flow meter. If we do things that increase the flow, such as getting support from others and changing our self-talk, then we will be enabling our physis to keep us developing.

Doing Feelings
– Making friends with ourselves –

IT'S OKAY!

Were you tempted to skip this chapter? Please don't. This section is practical, so stick with it – we're not going to do anything silly like hug a pillow or hold hands in a circle. We're going to *do* feelings, and that's okay.

We all have feelings. We are all thinking, feeling people who have hormones and biological processes swilling around inside us. However, we all have a different response to the word 'feelings' and might shuffle uncomfortably when talking or reading about them, or thinking about what's going on deep inside us. For example, do you:

- Cry easily?
- Notice when other people need support?
- Acknowledge when you're hungry, or do you carry on working?
- Share your feelings openly?

- Think that people with feelings are showing weakness?
- Run away from a conversation when someone asks how you're feeling?

We all have our own views on feelings and we have learnt which ones are safe to show and when it is safe to show them. Sometimes we might get caught out when overwhelmed by emotion: at a funeral or the birth of a child, for example. When this happens we might scold ourselves for 'being silly' and do our best to hide our tears, or we might just let it all out and allow them to run freely.

Whatever our feelings are and how we respond to them, it's healthy to give them due consideration so that they don't sabotage our efforts to bounce back.

GRRRRR! ARRRGH!

Let's not pretend that bouncing back is a jolly stroll in the park where we move from one slightly less pleasant piece of lawn to one slightly more pleasant piece. No. It's more like we're walking through the park and suddenly realise that we've crossed a boundary into a neighbouring field and have trodden in a giant cowpat, made by the entire herd clubbing together and producing such a whopper that you could lose a digger in there. At this moment we're likely to shout profanities and feel like the world has, yet again, done it to us. It has. Horrid world – it's full of pat-dumping cows and in order to survive and thrive we need to hold our breath. And then we need to let it out again.

By hold our breath I mean that we have to react to the situation and that often means coping for a while until we can make sense of it. The day after I lost my job for the first time I started to get ready for work and my girlfriend said:

'Where are you going?'

'Um... to work?' I replied sarcastically.

'What work?' she asked pleasantly.

'Oh.'

The reality of my situation dawned on me. I had become 'one of *those* people' that we read about in the press – someone whose job had been made redundant and who was now part of the national statistics. That didn't feel very nice. In fact, it was humiliating. How could they treat me like that? What were my friends going to say? Where was my next job coming from? I didn't know. All I knew was that I had to face the world sometime, but not today – today I was just too full of overwhelming feelings to do anything constructive.

THE TRUTH ABOUT FEELINGS

People often shy away from talking about what's going on inside them, because they don't want to appear 'silly' or 'weak', even when their body language suggests that they're one large coffee away from a heart attack or a meltdown. We need to remember that:

1. **Feelings won't go away if we ignore them**. If we feel hungry, for example, but push the feeling away and carry on working, the pangs will still surface again in a short while.
2. **Feelings are a perfectly normal part of human behaviour.** Their quantity, duration and intensity can vary of course, but they are part of our life.
3. **Feelings can't really be 'seen'.** Just because our work colleague seems cool and calm doesn't mean that he or she isn't panicking on the inside. Likewise, a job interviewer can't see what's really going on inside us. We can look for clues and infer what might be happening for someone else, but we never know for certain.

4. **Feelings can influence our health.** If we are stressed, for example, we might have a migraine when the stress is lifted. Migraines are sometimes called 'Saturday headaches' for that reason, because we spend the whole week keeping the bad thoughts at bay and when we relax during the weekend, they creep out and cause a nuisance.

5. **Feelings are there to help us.** They grab our attention and help us to focus. Fear, for example, alerts us to re-think our actions or make sure we're properly secured before we leap into space!

6. **Feelings can be rediscovered.** Just because we had a family environment that encouraged us to push our feelings away and 'keep going', or as one friend told me 'to suck it up buttercup', that doesn't mean we can't learn to reconnect with our feelings again.

7. **Feelings are ours.** We may be influenced by others who have told us how we should feel, but although they meant well, it's up to us to lead our lives and feel our feelings – we make our own choices!

SPOTTING FEELINGS

How do we know what is really happening inside us? Feelings keep us safe from harm, they help us to come to terms with loss, they provide us with energy for action and they allow us to experience situations around us. The problem is that we can easily push them aside and carry on until it's too late and we have a breakdown, fall asleep at the wheel of our car, or explode with rage and hurt someone we love. We learn to hide our feelings, to cover them up and to use socially acceptable phrases – such as 'Oh, I'm all right really, just a bit tired that's all' – to avoid conversations about what we are really feeling. People often ask us how we feel and all they expect is a friendly answer that doesn't require any work on their part, so we quickly learn to play along instead of replying truthfully:

'Oh I'm so glad you asked. I'm terrified at the prospect of losing my job and would really like to talk to you about it.'

As a result of this we can fall out of practice at acknowledging our feelings and talking honestly about them. In order to improve how we do feelings we need to recognise the clues that point to internal seismic activity. Which ones do you do?

CLUES FOR WHEN WE'RE FEELING STRESSED

1) **Tiredness.** If we feel leaden and readily fall asleep then we might be feeling miserable or scared. Taking ourselves 'offline' is nature's way of protecting us.

2) **Outbursts.** If we find ourselves snapping at those around us then we're probably feeling anxious and the anger is more about us failing to reign in our feelings than it is about someone making a mistake.

3) **Inactivity.** Attempting to make a drink and finding ourselves immobile, staring into space, is a sign that we are processing something internally and possibly wishing to be in a different place.

4) **Tapping.** If we are drumming our fingers or discreetly tapping a foot then it's likely that we have energy inside us percolating up from a feeling and we need to find an outlet for it. This can be a precursor to an outburst, so if we do find ourselves tapping it's perhaps time to get up and go for a walk.

5) **Compliance**. We go along with what's being asked of us, despite a nagging sense that this isn't what we want to do. Perhaps we are feeling scared about speaking out and have decided to toe the line for now in order to avoid confrontation.

6) **Over-compensating**. If we enjoy having a drink or a cigarette, in times of stress we may find that we like to smoke twice as much or perhaps find ourselves opening a second bottle of wine. We might assure ourselves that it's to help us get to sleep, but there are better ways of resting than by getting drunk.

7) **Headaches**. Our bodies respond to the release of adrenalin and related hormones and if we can't dissipate them through the classic fight or flight response then our body might find other ways to alert us to what is going on. Some people get headaches, others suffer from insomnia, skin rashes or dietary intolerance. These physical symptoms are often linked to stress, which can be caused by anger at the way we're being treated and the fear of what the future holds.

8) **New behaviour.** When things get tough we might suddenly find ourselves developing habits that are out of character. Perhaps we start going for long walks, or get in our car and drive around aimlessly, or find that we have to read a series of books, or run until we fall down from exhaustion. If our loved ones are telling us that we are doing odd new things then take note – we are probably in a worse state than we realise.

9) **Saying *No* or *But*.** When we're struggling it's likely that we will be offered well-meaning and practical advice, suggestions and a range of steps we can take to help us. If we hear ourselves repeatedly saying 'no, I'm too busy this week' or 'I would like to go to that meeting, but I'm already committed' then we're fooling ourselves. We could make the time if we wanted to, but tend not to, probably because we're a bit scared. We can say 'yes' and get some support. It's okay to ask for help: Nobody wins a gold medal at a sporting event without benefitting from help and guidance.

If you're unsure about which, if any, clues apply to you then show them to a trusted friend or partner and ask them for their opinion. Feedback is useful because what we think of as 'a little snooze' might be us being comatose on the sofa all evening.

DOING FEELINGS IS USEFUL

There are four suggested 'base feelings' which underpin all the other words that we might use to describe how we feel at a given moment in time: *happy, sad, angry* and *scared*. Interestingly, while feelings are internal processes, how we respond to them can be conditioned by our external environment and by the rules and levels of tolerance that others allow. Think about the last time you cried, or confided in someone about being scared. Were there other times when you felt those feelings but didn't feel able to tell people, perhaps worried about their response?

We need to have access to all our feelings because they provide us with useful information. If we are going to set up a business, for example, we will think carefully and work out our finances, design a product, choose a name and sort out a logo for our business card. All of this work is informed by feelings, because the feeling is 'father to the thought'. Although we might not overtly consider or show them, now that we're in the process of bouncing back we need to do some feeling, so that we can make sense of our thoughts, untangle what is knotted inside us and release pent up frustrations.

DOING SADNESS

We often learn to hide the sadness we feel as a child, and perhaps cover it up with anger. When something is removed from us, we feel sad at the loss. It's okay to feel sad that our job has been taken from us, that our work colleagues are just friends now, or that our business has come to an end. We might feel 'heavy' with sadness and instead of replacing it with anger, we can find someone to talk to and let it out of us. If it's hard to talk to our partner then we can spend time with a trusted friend, or with a coach or counsellor. Feeling our sadness and coming to terms with it will allow us to move forward – whereas many people hang on their sadness and wallow because they get attention for what they have lost, rather than grieving properly and then being praised for what they later achieve.

DOING FEAR

We often get scared as a child: On our first day at school, the night before exams, sleeping in a strange room on holiday, waiting to be scolded after breaking something… The unfamiliar, the risky and the fear of consequences all give us good grounds to be scared. Some people talk about their fear, others admit to being scared and get help or seek advice, others hold on to it and pretend all is well when it isn't. I've worked with many people in the middle of transitioning and in my experience it is fear that causes the most problems in terms of progress. People are scared that they won't know what to do, that they will make a mistake, that they will lose something on the journey or that they will change negatively. The fear holds them back and although they appear to do a good job of planning for the future, learning new skills and saying the right things, inside they know it's an act – so they sabotage themselves in order to stay where they are. The unpleasantness of their current situation is outweighed by the fear of moving forward.

If you're reading this and smiling at your secret fear, then it is okay to be worried and to admit it. People often hide fear behind *confusion* and instead of making progress they repeatedly ask questions, but fail to grasp the task. In reality they know full well what to do, they're just too frightened to do it. We need to find a supporter who will take care of us by showing us what to do, by accompanying us on a visit, or by reassuring us over the telephone when we feel anxious.[13]

DOING ANGER

There is a myth that anger should be avoided and that it is not healthy to be cross or to vent our frustrations. Well, I beg to differ. If anger is used to cover up sadness, then that isn't honest and we need to stop, take a deep breath and then tell people what we are really feeling. Genuine anger though is different and can be a tremendously useful asset, because it can power our activities by releasing a huge tidal wave of physis. We feel anger if we have been wronged in some way. When the injustice we have received burns

[13] Several years ago I was invited to deliver a technical presentation and as I was a relatively inexperienced student at the time I asked my friend Joe to come with me. If he could find the venue for me and help set things up, then I would have less to worry about and could focus on my presentation. Joe made all the difference and the day was a great success. I would have baulked at a solo performance, but having a friend there made me feel safer and was reassuring.

inside us we have a choice: we can either let it overwhelm us and simply lash out, we can grumble and get attention for our misery, or we can do something positive.

THE TWO-STAGE ANGER ATTACK

The two-stage anger attack is so named because we have two tasks to complete in order to effectively harness our anger by attacking it head-on.

STAGE ONE – DEALING WITH 'SURFACE' ANGER

The first thing to do is to get rid of the raw nature of the external anger sitting close to the surface of our psyche. This requires us to undertake some kind of physical action to release pent up frustration:

- Go for a run.
- Walk briskly for as long as we need to.
- Play tennis or squash (where we can really smash the ball about).
- Scribble really hard on a pad of paper.
- Smack a punch bag.
- Go the gym and work out.
- Throw eggs against a wall.

A friend recommended this recipe as a very satisfying way of releasing anger: Take a dozen eggs, one wall and a piece of chalk. With the chalk, mark a large circle on the wall to aim for. Take ten steps away from the wall and throw each egg as hard as you can. Savour each egg, feel it in your hand, focus your anger at the spot on the wall and throw hard, preferably letting out a howl of rage as you do. It's a great way to release our pent-up frustrations.

STAGE TWO – DEALING WITH 'DEEP' ANGER

This level of anger is longer lasting and provides us with a more even source of energy than the rough surface anger that needs to be soothed quickly. Our deep anger is the embedded sense of wrong that we feel and we know that we can't rush to resolve the situation. We can, however, harness the energy it creates by setting ourselves a challenging task to complete that requires sustained effort. This might include:

- Completing a tough piece of work that we have been delaying.
- Spending a week really focussing on establishing our next business or getting our job-hunting programme fully established.
- Working on a cherished project that we never had the time for before.
- Setting a tough deadline to finish decorating the house or fixing our car.
- Entering a competition and working methodically to ensure we do well in it.

Our project doesn't necessarily have to be directly work-related. We are using this opportunity to do something to be proud of, to show ourselves what we are capable of and to complete something significant, which requires thought and a higher level of commitment. That's why the deadlines count, because we can use our energy to achieve a goal in a relatively short period of time and therefore move forward from our current position into a new place. In my case I was so angry once that I wrote an entire book over a four-week period. I typed and typed and the words rushed out headlong and in an untidy pile, but at the end of the project I did have a book, however scruffy it might have been.

- What would you like to achieve?
- What can you really push yourself to do?

You probably have something your heart desires and now you have permission to go for it. It's all part of bouncing back because dealing with our anger will help us to progress through the stages of the High-Cs transition model.

DOING HAPPINESS

This is about genuine happy feelings and not anti-sadness where we pretend to be happy by rebelling and enjoying ourselves in a hedonistic outpouring of partying, drinking and wild abandon. We might want to let off some steam, but we need to be careful that we're not simply masking our unhappiness with extreme 'positive' behaviour.

When was the last time you really felt happy? When was there joy in your heart and a smile on your face? (When you didn't mind the rain, the noise from the children or the pile of work in front of you?)

Cleaning our house when we're miserable is a thankless chore, but when we're excited at the prospect of a visitor then it becomes part of the fun of preparing for the enjoyable times ahead. It's the same with our modern career – the workload is always lighter when we're happier and heavier when we're dragging sadness along behind us. We can think about real happiness as a lightness in our step and a sense that all is well and that the little knocks and bumps don't matter. This is happiness. It can't be bought, stolen or faked. There's one tip here: *do what makes you genuinely happy*.

TRANSITION FEELINGS

We can add to the High-Cs model from the earlier chapter and think about what sort of feelings are likely to be experienced in each stage. The table below shows the sort of general feelings we might encounter, together with the underlying feeling that relates to them. As we move though the stages we will experience a range of feelings and cover all four of the underlying feelings – even if we don't use those exact words to describe them.

TRANSITION STAGE	KEY ACTIVITY	LIKELY FEELINGS
1) Stressful Chaos	The bad stuff is happening right now!	Fear (scare) as we need to take care of ourselves
2) Tense Calm	It's over. Something has gone, been lost or changed	Relief (happy) that it's over, mixed with anxiety (scare) at what might follow and longing (sadness) at what might have been

3) Free Cleansing	Letting go of the past and tidying up our world	Cross (anger) at the way we were treated, mixed with pleasure (happy) at letting go of baggage
4) Anxious Consideration	Fact-finding and planning, thinking about consequences	Nervous (scare) at the uncertainty of the future
5) Hopeful Catching	Beginning the next stage of our modern career	Anxiety (scare) at what is to come, blended with frustration (anger) at wanting to reach a new goal. Possibly some excitement too (happy) as we're finally heading off in a new direction
6) Careful Coordination	Making progress and adjusting our course	Anxiety (scare) over whether we're heading in the right direction
7) Joyful Celebration	Celebrating progress made and way-points ticked off	Content and relaxed (happy) that we have really done well and have either bounced back, or are beginning to achieve a significant change in our fortunes

CASE STUDY – ANDREW

I once worked with a very senior manager whose performance had slipped badly. His host organisation was in a dilemma. On the one hand he was hindering their efforts to realise the value from a project, because he wasn't delivering agreed milestones on time. On the other hand when he performed to his ability he was brilliant and produced very high quality value-adding work on a consistent basis. To resolve the dilemma I was invited to work with Andrew and establish what we could do to make progress.

After we had spent time together as a coach and client for a couple of sessions and had built a high level of trust we started to explore what was happening at a deeper level. Andrew revealed how bad the situation was making him feel: it was giving him health problems, which meant he was underperforming, leading to increased stress and in turn, more health problems. It was a vicious circle and one that he had been in denial about for some time – a classic sign he was in the *Stressful Chaos* stage of transition and was just too scared to admit what a tough place he had got himself into. The admission of his genuine health issue provided me with an essential insight that I could use to raise his awareness:

'Andrew,' I said, 'it's okay to be sick and to take of yourself. And it's okay to be scared about your job – because the fact is that if you don't improve they *will* get rid of you.'

I didn't know this for a fact, but his manager had hinted strongly that this was being discussed, despite giving Andrew a supportive message that 'all would be well'. My friendly concern mixed with the reality of the situation bypassed his usual protection by denial and overwhelmed, he broke down and sobbed. I let him cry it out and then smiled at him:

'Nice work,' I said, by way of friendly reassurance, 'now that you're in touch with your real feelings we can stop pretending this isn't a serious career-ending situation and can make progress.'

And we did. We recontracted with his manager, changed his working pattern and he used the new regime to get well and improve his performance. Without him uncovering his real feelings he might have carried on in denial and would probably have been asked to leave.

KEEP REVISITING FEELINGS

We can read this chapter and quickly forget about it and move on. Or we can allow ourselves to understand that all feelings are okay and that doing feelings is an essential underpinning of success. If we don't get in touch with them, it's likely that we will sabotage our progress in some way as fear outweighs the possibly of progress, or anger paralyses us in a drunken haze. We can keep revisiting our feelings, throw more eggs and keep talking to people so that the hurt is soothed, the injustice is listened to and our fed-up inner person is properly heard. Keep coming back to this chapter until the wounds have healed and you have a smile on your face.

SUMMARY & NEW HABIT #8

Summary

We can run away from our feelings, but they will catch up with us again. We can pretend that we're not scared but we're only fooling ourselves. We can allow anger to get the better of us or we can harness its power to propel us forward. Feelings are useful and help us to make quality decisions, think twice about taking a risk or guide us when we're not sure which way to go. If doing feelings feels a little nervous to you, then find a friend and make them your trusted buddy for the transition. All you need to do is talk to them and invite them to listen.

OUR NEW HABIT TO HELP US BOUNCE BACK:

- Notice the signs that we have a feeling lurking inside us. Perhaps we are snappy, or overly tired, or are resisting an invitation that could help us. If we notice our external behaviour, we can deal with what is happening inside us and take steps to work with our feelings for our benefit.

Buying Time

– Increasing horizons to reduce panic –

THE BIGGEST WORRY

One of the feelings that we are likely to experience is panic – the sense that life has spun out of control and presented us with a heap of worry, of which the largest slice is going to be money. Do we have enough? How long will it last? What happens if we run out? These are the kind of questions that keep us awake at night as we make sense of our new situation and come to terms with the fact that although we have many tasks to do to plan our career, take care of ourselves and so on, we have one fundamental task to attend to right away – namely manage our money, to keep the lights on and food in the fridge.

CASE STUDY – ADAM

Adam was in a tough spot because he had been suspended by his organisation pending a disciplinary process that a dictator would have been proud of. Fair, reasonable and based on facts – it wasn't. However, while the Human Resources department were combing through old emails looking for evidence of significant wrongdoing (of which there was none) Adam was at home, with little to do but fret the time away and wait to be summoned. In all probability the 'disciplinary process' was just a vicious way of saving money, as the organisation had a reputation for finding fault with senior executives and then bullying them into accepting an offer to 'leave on good terms'. However, Adam had to plan for two eventualities:

- Being fired and leaving with only basic entitlements, or
- Being offered a compromise agreement.

He wasn't sleeping and was beginning to panic that if he was fired his house would have to be sold. When we're panicking it's likely that our thinking is shoved to one side as raw adrenaline takes over and we lose sight of the facts. In this case I asked a few standard questions during a session to focus Adam's attention:

THINKING ABOUT MONEY

1. How much do you have in savings?
2. What other liquid assets (cash) can you get hold of?
3. How much money will you receive from your ex-employer?
4. What can you do to take a mortgage payment holiday (with the permission of the bank)?
5. How much is owed on your credit card?
6. What non-essential expenditure can you immediately stop/delay/reduce?
7. What else can you reduce/replace/cut in order to run your household at an absolute minimum for three months?
8. What shopping/lifestyle habits need to change to support this period?

> 9. Who else can you ask for support, in case of an emergency?
> 10. What other 'unthinkable' options are helpful to think about now?

In Adam's case he realised that he had savings, he had used a small bonus to over-pay his mortgage and his monthly expenditure was relatively low. He grumbled that he didn't want to spend any of his savings to keep food in the fridge, which is a classic situation. Nobody wants to work hard and see their savings used up on commodity purchases. However, using savings to buy food is much more sensible than using them to buy a new television, given the choice, and if savings have been prudently accrued for a rainy day then we can congratulate ourselves on a job well done.

'It's now raining,' I said to Adam, 'and that's what your savings are for. You don't have to spend them yet, just factor them into your thinking because they will buy you time.'

He agreed and relaxed. He then realised that if he added in a mortgage repayment holiday he could reduce his family's living expenses to provide them with a 12-month time horizon before they would have to cut more drastically. He relaxed a bit more and smiled. The process of checking out the facts and seeing the resources he had at hand enabled his time horizon to increase from 'we'll have to sell the house in three months' to 'we could last a year and see where we are then'.

HOW MUCH TIME DO WE NEED TO BUY?

The answer is, sadly, always more than we think we need. Have a look at the timetable and see where you fit in and how it compares to your initial estimate and financial reality:

(A) TAKING TIME TO FIND A JOB	(B) TAKING TIME TO BUILD A BUSINESS
• 0 – 3 months, if we're exceptionally well connected. • 3 – 6 months if we're exceptionally proactive and network like our life depends on it. • 6 – 12 months for the general population who seek job-hunting support. • 6 – 18 months for the general population who just trust to luck and who have no particular job-hunting skills. • 12 – 18 months for people who are hit hard by the loss of their previous role and despite good intentions, struggle to get moving for the first 6 months.	• 0 – 6 months to find a small piece of consultancy work or short interim position, if our specialisation is in demand and we go networking. • 6 – 12 months to find a consultancy contract or to begin selling products/ services through our trading business.[14] • 12 – 24 months to break even if we are running a new start-up business. • 24 – 36 months to begin generating a small profit in our start-up business.

Please don't think that 0 – 6 months means you have a good chance of bouncing out of one job straight into another. It tends to mean 4 – 6 months, i.e. it will probably take most of the 6 months to sort yourself out, *unless* you have a lucky strike with an initial

---

[14] It often takes 6 months to find corporate clients. If we open a shop we might start selling right away, but it will still take time to become sustainable. Making our first sale feels fantastic, but it doesn't make a business.

job application. In business we have to account for the fact that the world is already full of interim people, consultants, service providers and new business start-ups. We can enter the market and work hard to be successful, but we will need to out-perform our established competitors. To be successful we need to be clear what makes us:

- Special
- Different
- Worth hiring instead of the other person
- Better than the competition.

What does 'better' mean? It might be that we sell similar products, but that we are much more effective networkers. Or that we might be a friendlier person to deal with, or we have a smarter way of packaging our products or a clever way to delight our customers. Offering 'freemium' items (free premium products) can be a good way to build trust and a sense that we provide good value.

Freemium items have a value to the customer and they get them for nothing as a way of introducing them to our products or services. Examples can include a sample of an ebook, a tasting sample in a café, a bag to carry folders in, a free game or app, a copy of additional workshop handouts, a few spare screws to help us out and so on. I remember that a builder once gave me a radiator key to help us bleed our new radiators. He didn't have to, but he had a spare and happily left it with us – this might have cost him nothing, but the small act of generosity was part of the evidence to us that he was a caring sort who looked after his customers. If we have time for the little things, it tends to suggest to customers that we will do a great job of getting the big things right.

CASE STUDY – COLIN

I was working with a client who seemed fairly sanguine about his imminent departure from a six-figure role with a bonus to match, and I was curious to find out why he was so relaxed, so I asked him. He grinned and replied:

'Well, Richard, I've decided to become a consultant. I have lots of contacts and people seem to like me, so it shouldn't be too difficult to find work.'

'What's your special skill,' I asked calmly, 'that if I was in your industry I would readily pay for?'

'Oh easy,' he said cheerily, 'I know lots about the machining industry.'

It was great to see his enthusiasm, but blind confidence can be a precursor to a chilling dose of reality. I suggested that 'knowing lots' wasn't a sufficiently good reason to hire him and that he would need to be clear what he was consulting about and what made him worth spending money on. He had an idealised image of a consultant and when we talked it through in detail he realised that his 'quick bounce' was, in all probability, going to take at least six months.

REMEMBER HOLIDAYS

Sadly not ours – I'm referring to public holidays. It's easy to assume that 'six months to find a job' means just that, but in practice it means six 'working' months, so we can remove August and December from our planning. Although the world doesn't entirely close down for a summer break or a Christmas party, it does slow down dramatically and organisations often go into a kind of stasis because key managers are either away, covering for colleagues, or running hard to meet end-of-season deadlines.

THINKING THE UNTHINKABLE

Part of successful financial planning and management is to be ruthless with money *today* so that we can have more flexibility tomorrow. We don't know how long it will take to begin earning money again and because of this we need to conserve as much cash as possible because:

- Things always take longer than we first realise
- Things are always more expensive than we have budgeted for.

Therefore, we need to make sure we are pragmatic with ourselves and those around us to ensure we survive. All the cash we spend now is money that we don't have available to use in the future, so we need to *think twice and spend once*.

We can start by listing all the non-essential items and making sure that we don't waste our cash on them. However, if we need things that will help us in our modern career, such as a new suit or a low-cost laptop and printer it does make sense to include them in our calculations. No matter how great your interview technique is, arriving for a job interview in jeans and a t-shirt is almost always going to result in failure.

THE CAR STORY

I made a mistake and I had to put it right. Over a few years I had saved up a reasonable amount of money and thinking that the crash of 2008/2009 was behind us and that business was gently recovering, I decided it was time to change my car. My much-loved Swedish saloon had clocked 185,000 miles and it was due for retirement. I had already delayed changing my car for a year when the credit crunch arrived and prudently kept my money 'safely' in the bank. However, in an optimistic frame of mind I decided to splash out and bought a racy German convertible that I liked very much. It was great fun to drive in the summer sun and the winter snow, day and night with the hood down and the wind in my hair. The only problem with this pleasure was that the business recovery was not happening as fast as I had thought. This meant the car spent too much time parked on the driveway and I spent too much time trying to justify its continued presence to my wife.

When I had purchased it I made a sincere promise that if the recovery stalled I would sell it again – and before I had owned the car for a year it went in for a service, which forced the issue. Faced with the expense of buying a set of new low-profile ultra-speedy and therefore ultra-expensive tyres, I decided on the spot that that was it. I sold the car, much to the relief of my wife, and purchased another smaller Swedish saloon car *and* received a cheque from the garage for the difference in price. My children were amazed, convinced that the garage was not only giving me a free car but was in fact paying me to drive it off the forecourt. Actually for a moment, I thought the same too, and it just underlined that it was the right thing to do.

Although it was a painful parting, a car is only a lump of metal and there is no point hanging on to it if we don't need it, or if we need to pump some cash into our business.

Having a smart car was great fun, but you can do more with food. It was a tough business decision, but it was one that I took and was proud to do so. That's my car story.

- What is *your* story going to be about?
- What tough decisions do you need to make?
- What do you need to sell, or delay purchasing?

If your company car has been returned, do not rush out and buy a car straight away. It might be cheaper to use public transport or even to hire a car for when you need it. Spending a lump of cash on a car or signing up for an expensive car loan is not a wise move on day one. Save the expenditure for day 101 when you know exactly what you need and can justify the purchase.

FORWARD-LOOKING CASH MANAGEMENT

In order to make sure that we have *what* we need *when* we need it, I strongly suggest producing a cashflow forecast, which shows what our financial life will look like over the next few months, so that we don't inadvertently run out of money. Once we have the numbers in place we can tweak things to see where we need to increase our income or reduce our spending. The added bonus is that all income we do receive, such as from consultancy work, freelancing, labouring or from shelf-stacking, can extend our time horizon into the future. If we have six months of savings and can earn the equivalent of one month of household expenditure during that time, we can survive for *seven* months. This is good news as the longer our time horizon is the more chance we have of properly bouncing back.[15]

Look at the forecast shown in Sample (A) on the following page. What do you notice? Would you manage your money like this and go overdrawn in April? There is an 'easy' fix here – we can take a more optimistic view of our planned income from casual work, and then the lack of funds in July is magically transformed into a handsome profit. This is a dangerous way to manipulate a forecast though, because income isn't certain, whereas expenditure almost always is – and that's what we have control of and need to reduce immediately.

[15] All forecasts are just a bad guess written down. They are not statements of absolute fact, so always proceed with caution. However, they are significantly more useful to us than a blank sheet of paper.

SAMPLE (A) – INITIAL CASH FLOW FORECAST

Month	Jan	Feb	Mar	Apr	May	Jun	Jul
Opening Bank Balance	0	2,250	1,000	250	-500	-1,250	-2,500
INCOME							
Redundancy payment	+2,000						
Withdraw savings	+1,500						
Planned casual work			+500	+500	+500		
EXPENSES							
Mortgage	-500	-500	-500	-500	-500	-500	-500
Food	-400	-400	-400	-400	-400	-400	-400
General household	-200	-200	-200	-200	-200	-200	-200
Taxes and utilities	-150	-150	-150	-150	-150	-150	-150
Closing Bank Balance	2,250	1,000	250	-500	-1,250	-2,500	-3,750

We don't want to over-inflate potential income because if we do and it fails to materialise we will have already spent our cash and will be left struggling to cope. This approach has been the death of many companies who assume that their sales forecast is more of a reality than a guess and as such commission expensive projects in order to begin the year on a positive note.

There's an old business saying that *'a sale is only a sale when their money is in your bank account'*. Until then it's just a *potential* sale. Securing sales can often be more problematic than we first envisaged and it may take longer to be fully paid than we thought would be the case when we closed the deal. A colleague of mine has had to devote a considerable amount of time recently to debt management when his 'safe' corporate clients unilaterally extended payment terms from 60 to 90 days and then to 120 days, placing him under immense pressure to find clever ways of managing his cash so that he could pay his staff.

BE RUTHLESS

We need to take a fresh look at our cashflow forecast and be ruthless with our expenditure, because it will create the time we need to bounce back. Take a look at Sample (B) below and compare it with Sample (A). What differences do you notice?

SAMPLE (B) – RUTHLESS CASH FLOW FORECAST

Month	Jan	Feb	Mar	Apr	May	Jun	Jul
Opening Bank Balance	0	2,950	2,400	1,850	1,450	1,050	650
INCOME							
Redundancy payment	+2,000						
Withdraw savings	+1,500						
Planned casual work				+150	+150	+150	Job!
EXPENSES							
Mortgage	-100	-100	-100	-100	-100	-100	-100
Food	-200	-200	-200	-200	-200	-200	-200
General household	-100	-100	-100	-100	-100	-100	-100
Taxes and utilities	-150	-150	-150	-150	-150	-150	-150
Closing Bank Balance	2,950	2,400	1,850	1,450	1,050	650	100

In this second forecast we have been ruthless and only put in what we need to. We have taken a mortgage re-payment 'holiday' and are only paying the interest on the debt. Talking to our mortgage provider might be an uncomfortable experience, but the people in your local branch live in the real world too and know what life is like. We won't be the first or the last person to be asking the same question that day.

In the model we have also reduced our monthly food bill by cutting out expensive luxuries and buying more fresh ingredients (often more cost-effective than high-fat, high-salt ready meals). We have reduced our general household expenditure by deferring purchases and only budgeting for essentials. Utilities and taxes remain the same as it's harder to use less electricity. It is possible to be greener, however, and the cumulative effects of switching off lights and taking quicker power-showers will help too.[16]

We have also been more cautious with the time and amount of our planned casual work, in case it takes longer to find a shelf-stacking job or similar. Note that in July we end the month with £100 in the bank – however, this is the month we begin our new full-time role, having secured it in June. We need to remember though that we will be paid 30 days in arrears and as such the money doesn't come into the forecast until *August* when our first pay cheque is paid into our account.

The Sample (B) model clearly makes life easier for us in the short term, even though it highlights the need to work quickly and effectively to secure casual work and find a full-time job. With a longer time horizon it is likely that we will be calmer and this tends to translate into more productive job-hunting activities, because we can be methodical and poised instead of rushing about in a desperate haste to find work.

---

[16] High-pressure mixer showers can use the same amount of water in 10 minutes as a 'medium' bath would. However, by using energy-efficient shower heads and reducing showering time the amount of water can be reduced considerably.

Although the numbers in the model are only there as a guide it is surprising how much we can reduce our outgoings when we take a tough stance. I would add that, from personal experience, facing up to the numbers is tough to begin with, but does bring a sense of peace once we know what our financial world looks like and what we have to do to succeed.

SUMMARY & NEW HABIT #9

Summary

Money is a precious and scarce commodity and we need to hang on to ours for as long as possible. We need to be proactive and thoughtful, take sensible decisions and keep a close eye on our bank balance and our monthly outgoings. By being cautious and prudent it's possible to reduce our initial panic at losing our job and to give ourselves enough time to focus on what we need to do to bounce back. Once we have secured a new role or managed to turn our business around then we can relax a bit and indulge in a few luxuries.

OUR NEW HABIT TO HELP US TO DEVELOP:

- Produce a cashflow forecast so that we can plan our income and expenditure for the next few months ahead, to help us stretch our resources as far as we can. However, simply 'having' a cashflow forecast isn't enough – we need to update it each month and make sure we only spend within our budget.

Thinking ABC

– Giving our brain a workout –

THINKING VS REACTING

We all think. We can't help it. However, we need to be sure of the facts before making a decision and consider the risks and consequences of our actions and inactions. This chapter is about ensuring that our thinking is robust enough to enable us to bounce back successfully, because it is highly likely that our thinking will be compressed under the weight of the pressure we feel and we may lose clarity. On a more positive note, once we have acknowledged our feelings, produced a cashflow forecast, increased our flow of physis and begun to plan the next stage of our modern career then we're already thinking at a higher level and can congratulate ourselves.

THINKING IS WORK

Taking time to think is an essential part of work. Sadly, organisations and managers often try to curtail thinking among their staff, restrict the free flow of information and focus on activity and output, rather than time spent analysing facts and creating options. Thinking is work – if we are going to bounce back (and we are) we need to give ourselves permission to spend time sitting quietly sketching ideas, scribbling notes and staring into space (so that our brain can freewheel a bit). Physical activities such as gardening, running or playing a musical instrument can help too, because as we devote energy to the obvious external activity, internally our cognitive processes will be making sense of and testing our ideas. Take time to think – it's cheaper than making a mistake.

CREATING OPTIONS

People often come up with an idea and then try hard to make it work even when it becomes obvious that it hasn't been fully thought through. When it is their only idea they *have* to make it work, because if it doesn't they don't have anything else to fall back on. Clearly, this is a hazardous way to try and bounce back, so it makes sense to create more options in order to reduce the risk.

Creating options is often easiest when working with a supporter, coach, mentor, partner, friend – anyone who will listen to us and give us the space to develop our ideas and who will prod us by asking:

- What else could we do?
- What are all the options available to us, however silly they might sound at first?
- What do other people already do?
- What is our secret wish, dream or ambition?
- If we sat with a blank piece of paper what else might we come up with?

We don't have to be in an office to create options – the most creative meetings I've been involved with have often taken place standing next to a flipchart, walking in a park or sitting in a café watching the world go by. Think about:

- Where do you like to do your creating thinking?
- What can you do to make thinking a fun experience?

THE IDEAS CLOCK

When generating more options we can use a clock-face approach to get a good breadth and depth of ideas and to encourage us to be more creative. It doesn't matter if we subsequently reject an idea – they all have value because they each inform our overall thinking in one way or another. To use the Ideas Clock we can start by writing the problem, the theme of our thinking, or the dilemma we are facing in the centre. Then we write our first idea or solution in the 12 o'clock position. A good tip is to notice our first thoughts because they often contain our preferred solutions. This is because we've been thinking about the answer for longer than we realise.

The next step is to write the opposite of that idea (or a radical alternative) in the 6 o'clock space so that we have a natural counterpoint. We can then tweak the first idea, using the prompts on the different parts of the clock face to pull and stretch it and give it a good 'workout'. There is also space to write fresh ideas on the clock face and once we have filled some or all of the 12 positions we know that we have generated options and broadened our thinking.

THE IDEAS CLOCK

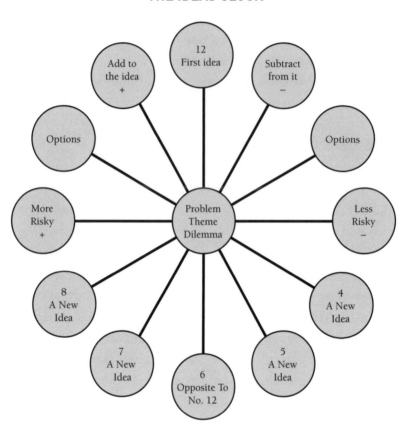

On the following page is an example to show how the clock approach can benefit our thinking. You are free to add or subtract spokes to suit your own needs – play with the model and tweak it so that it works for you.

WORKED EXAMPLE FOR MY BUSINESS START-UP

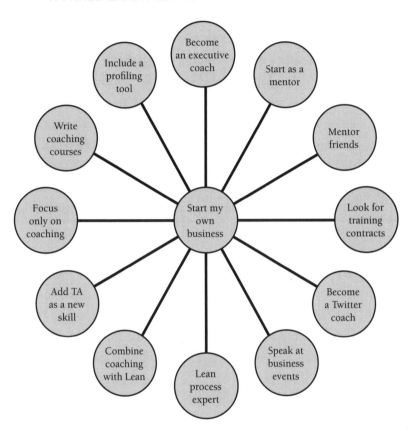

THE FACET PROCESS FOR GOOD DECISION-MAKING

When we have a key decision to make it is helpful to follow a process, because good processes give rise to great outcomes. By using the FACET model we can pay more attention to the essential process stages, which will make our final decision more robust.

The Facet Process comprises five stages:

1. **Find Facts.** We can mix objective information with subjective guesses if we need to, as long as we know which are which

and account for inherent assumptions. By researching the costs, timescales, complexities and risks associated with a decision we will move out of a merely feeling-and-reacting state and into a more grounded, thoughtful one.[17]

2. **Analyse Results.** Simply gathering information is not enough: we need to search for patterns, trends and clues to guide us. Numbers can easily overwhelm us, so the key is to remain focussed on the big picture and ask ourselves if the figures show an improvement or a decline. Do the numbers support or dispute our initial ideas? If they dispute them, we need to understand why, instead of simply discarding unhelpful information.

3. **Conclude Research.** We need to stop our analyses, take a step back and ask ourselves: So what? Now that we have given the data a good shake and scrutinised them to our satisfaction, what is the outcome? If we were a journalist about to file a story, what would the headline be? If we were explaining the conclusion to an eight-year-old child, what would we say?[18]

4. **Evaluate Impact.** Once we have drawn conclusions from our work so far we can relate it to the decision we are about to make. Is there a preferred option that now presents itself, or has an uncomfortable truth been unearthed that puts our plan into disarray? If this is the case, we need to generate more options and repeat the process up to this point.

5. **Take Decisions.** Assuming that the facts support our plan and we are happy with the outcome we can now take our decision. It's worth noting that *not* taking a decision can still have consequences that we need to factor into our thinking.

---

[17] Feelings are great and will tend to give us a more general direction to head in, which can be refined by the inclusion of key facts.
[18] Talking to an imaginary eight-year-old child is a good way to cut through the fog, or to avoid hiding behind complex technical language.

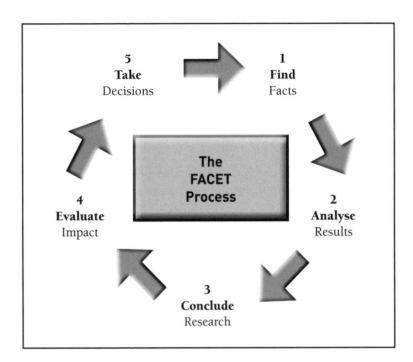

FACET CASE STUDY – PRINTING VS COACHING

As an example of the FACET process in action, some years ago I wanted to buy a small print business. It looked like a fun thing to do – I had a background in print and the idea of owning my own business was appealing. I talked to the vendor and looked at the accounts (Find Facts), which seemed to indicate that the business was ticking along, but would be hard to grow without significant investment. To double-check my thinking, I showed the accounts to a finance director friend of mine (Analyse Results), who laughed and said: 'No way!' The numbers were just not going to add up to a successful enterprise for me and I politely declined the opportunity (Conclude Research). The impact on my thinking though was to realise that I didn't really have the technical skills to run a small print business and that I didn't want the complexity of looking after stock and machinery (Evaluate Impact). I wanted a simple business that I could excel at, so instead I invested in me – I signed up for coaching training and headed off in a different direction (Take Decisions).

I was also forced to confront a deeper truth. My first idea had been to work as a coach and an organisational development specialist and for a moment the print business seemed to be the safe and easy option – buy a little business and instantly become successful. Of course, I was wrong. There is no instant route to success and if I hadn't followed the FACET process I could have made a catastrophic decision.

AIM FOR GROUNDED THINKING

When endeavouring to think clearly we can find ourselves inadvertently succumbing to sneaky bugbears that sit outside our awareness and trip us up. Although we might *think* that we're thinking clearly, chances are we're being guided by an unseen force, such as the views of close friends and relatives, or our own unspoken prejudices and concerns. There's no shame in falling foul of a bugbear... the trick is to remember they exist, befriend them and make sure we're acting in awareness. Here are the more common ones. Which do you do?

FIVE THINKING BUGBEARS

Which ones get in the way of your thinking?

1. **Impulsive enthusiasm.** This is great when we need it, but it can get us into trouble when let loose. We need to rein it in when we want to think clearly.

---

2. **Rebellion.** We might look like we're thinking positively and actively trying to problem solve, when in fact we are deciding to rebel and follow a different path. This might be fun for a while, but we risk allowing our pique to get in the way of the facts. In this case it can help to reread the chapter about Doing Feelings and find ways to properly express our anger and frustration at the situation we find ourselves in.

3. **Influence from others.** We might have 'voices' in our head that say we cannot do certain things, or that doing this is 'silly' and we *should* do something else instead. When we notice a voice, or an echo of a parent, partner or friend, we need to stop and let the voice go quiet. We can decide for ourselves what we want to do.[19]

4. **Hasty thinking.** We make a lightning-fast pass of the facts and jump to a conclusion, maybe pretending that we have thought things through enough to justify our actions. Good practice is to give ourselves proper reflection time – if we make the decision on a Monday make sure we don't actually enact it until Tuesday. That way we can at least sleep on it and see if we still think the same way in the morning.

5. **Archaeology.** This is when we think so deeply about something that it's as if we're digging a hole and looking for buried treasure... and we can get bit lost and forget the world around us. If we are spending too much time assembling every last fact and acquiring copious amounts of background information, we need to pause and think about what the problem is here – are we looking for reassurance? What are we worried about?

---

[19] If we hear ourselves saying 'what I should do is...' we need to stop and ask where that voice came from. Was it a father figure telling us what is good for us? Or a mother figure being over-protective?

Consider this question:
- If your partner or close friend was reading this list, what would they say you tend to do sometimes?

THE ROLE OF INTUITION

Intuition is useful and we can learn to trust it to facilitate our forward progress. We often take decisions based on 'gut instinct'– something feels right to us and that's when we're accessing our intuition. A blend of prior experience, logical thought and informed guesswork, our intuition is there to guide us. We know from prior experience that a red ring on a cooker is probably too hot to touch, that a brick house will be stronger than a wooden one and that if we don't eat or sleep for days on end we are likely to fall over at some point.

If we're in a new situation, our intuition might be great as a general guide, but not so good when looking at the fine detail – hence the need to find a few facts and test our hunches. Our 'business intuition' can also be skewed by clever marketing. For example, studies suggest that if we're offered two similar products and one is more expensive than the other, our intuition is that the more expensive one is of better quality. In business though we need to be objective and make sure that what purports to be better quality doesn't just have a hefty mark-up.

If we look at the car industry for example, the top companies own several brands that all have a different marketplace position, but are in fact often built on the same production lines with many of the same parts. The body styles may differ, but the wiring behind the facade is often the same. The marketing campaigns reinforce brand differences and we inculcate these into our sense of differentiation. When see two different brands in a garage we intuitively select the one that feels right for us – but is that really intuition or just clever marketing?

Intuition is powerful and plays a useful role in helping us to bounce back. We can harness it to help our thinking on the condition that if we also have the slightest doubt we stop and assess the reality of the situation using grounded thinking.

SUMMARY & NEW HABIT #10

Summary

We need to give ourselves space and time to think clearly so that we make sensible decisions that support our overall career goals. We can use a process to help organise random thoughts into a coherent pattern and we can learn to intercept the thinking bugbears that might sneak up on us and cloud our judgement.

OUR NEW HABIT TO HELP US BOUNCE BACK:

- Celebrate the time we spend thinking as *productive* time. If we share the results of our deliberations with others and show them our notes they will know we have been using our time wisely and will encourage us to do even more thinking. And remember, we do have to pause our thinking eventually and take proactive decisions.

What's The Opportunity?

– Seeing the market –

IT'S A FUZZY WORLD

Top business people often comment that the key to success is about first seeing the opportunity and then secondly seizing it, so this chapter is going to focus on how we can open our eyes wider and 'see' the world more clearly. The next chapter will then help us to grab the opportunity and make something of it. However, if there was a magic formula for 'seeing opportunities' then life would be simple, because all we'd have to do is look around us and notice all the new prospects – like a sort of augmented reality for business. Sadly it's never that straightforward – the world is 'fuzzy' and the opportunities may be blurred and harder to spot. But there are things that we can do to help ourselves.

HOW TO CREATE OPPORTUNITIES

In order to bounce back we need to create new opportunities, be they ones that make us money, increase our knowledge, create leisure time or 'oddball' ones where we don't really know where they are taking us, but they feel like the right thing to be doing. We have to put some energy into the world in order for new opportunities to come back at us. *Creating* is an active process that requires us to keep practicing, so that we continue to populate our lives with a stream of new and interesting opportunities. Here are my top ten suggestions on how to create opportunities, and as you read through them, ask yourself which ones you really need to do more of:

---

10 WAYS TO CREATE OPPORTUNITIES:

1. **Increase the number of contacts we have.** We can do this by networking at social events, going to business groups, joining a club or utilising social media platforms to make new contacts.

2. **Talk to people.** Simply having contacts will not suffice. We need to engage them, perhaps by chatting with them on the internet and arranging to meet up for a coffee. Friendly chats are a great way to make new friends and broaden our horizons for new opportunities.

3. **Ask for something.** People can't read minds and so will not know what we're looking for. We need to be proactive and tell them what it is we're seeking.

4. **Listen to others.** If we pay attention in our conversations, we will hear people telling us about their problems or issues, and we might be able to help them out. Similarly if we keep an eye on the social media space and see someone reaching out for help we can respond to it. At the minimum we might make a new friend, and at best it could lead to an interesting business opportunity.

5. **Say 'Yes'.** It's tempting to filter people and their offers by getting nervous and saying 'no' too quickly. Instead, we can accept their offer and see where it takes us.

6. **Read trade magazines.** These are often full of job advertisements, articles and general trade adverts and you never know what you may find. We can send an introductory letter to the ones that catch our eye and see what response we get.

7. **Update our profile.** We need to make sure we have a current business or calling card that we can hand out. We also need to update our biographies on all the social media sites we use, because people do read them and will often respond positively if we're offering what they need.

8. **Visit exhibitions.** Local business exhibitions and open events often attract a wide cross-section of people. They can be well worth attending as a quick conversation can be followed up later that week with an invitation for coffee and a longer chat.

9. **Join a networking group.** There are lots of these around and they all have different styles, so we can choose ones that most appeal to us. We can join relevant special interest groups on LinkedIn and spend time with local business groups, trade bodies or professional organisations.

10. **Make an offer.** When conversing with contacts we can generate an opportunity by making them an offer. For example, if we offer our expertise in return for theirs (called a skill-swap), we create an opportunity for both parties to develop. Or, if we have two products to sell and our customer is used to buying the first one, we create the opportunity for them to buy something else by talking about our other product.

CASE STUDY – PAUL

Paul was a highly paid solicitor in a busy city centre office and after working long days and weekends decided that he had had enough. His health was suffering and he knew that he couldn't continue at this pace for much longer and decided to change his life completely. In order to create space for change he rented out his city flat and rented a cottage in the countryside.

He took time to allow his health to recover and began to think about what he could do next for work. Realising that he had had enough of law but didn't know enough to set up a small business, he began by drawing up a list of supporters and friends he could call on and then systematically met up with them or had lengthy telephone calls. One of them suggested he consider a franchise option as a way of getting into business. Intrigued, he visited a franchising fair, where he met lots of different businesses and talked to the vendors. In the end he purchased a business networking franchise and set up a website and a monthly meeting group to promote it. He's now very much enjoying himself as he always liked networking and chatting to people, so the business was a good fit for him. When he started he had no idea that this was where he would end up – however, by creating opportunities for himself he found a new and interesting direction to head in.

CASE STUDY – CHARLOTTE

Charlotte is a sous chef, responsible for managing the breakfast service in a busy local hotel and assisting the chef with the lunch service. I met her after she had lost her previous job and was finding it difficult to secure work despite being a good worker and someone who enjoyed the role. She had lost her way and couldn't see how to be proactive and create opportunities for herself. We began by reworking her CV and listing the various dishes she could cook, so a prospective employer could instantly get a sense of what she was confident in preparing and how she might fit in with his brigade. Once we had a great CV she drove around the area to all the hotels and pubs that she liked the look of and left copies for the owners and chefs to read. The next step was for her to practice her dishes because in a career such as cooking the interview is often less about talking and more about doing. Sure enough, her CV gained considerable interest because it was smart, informative and showed where she could add value. Charlotte was invited for several interviews and, with her confidence boosted by constant practice at home, soon joined the staff of a local hotel. She had been resourceful and sought help and then been proactive in order to create an opportunity for herself.

WHAT ARE WE ATTRACTED TO?

The process of bouncing back is often an emergent one, which means that we don't tend to have a complete route mapped out at the beginning. In Paul's example above, he knew what he didn't want to do and although he didn't know exactly what sort of business he wanted to be involved in he let his intuition guide him at the franchise fair. It can help us to focus our thinking by taking time to work out roughly what things we like – I mean 'roughly' too because in the early stages of generating opportunities we want to create a reasonably wide field of view.

To work out what we're attracted to we can take stock of our key skills, reflect on the people whose work interests us and consider general aspects of work that we find enjoyable. Take a moment to write a few points in the table on the following page and start to get a sense of where new opportunities might be waiting for you:

SKILL AUDIT TABLE

(1) Key work-related skills and areas of expertise	(2) Other trades or businesses that we find interesting	(3) General aspects of work that engage us and that we enjoy doing
Example: 1. Leadership expert 2. Sales skills	Example: 1. Friend who runs a flower shop 2. Colleague who retrained as a school teacher	Example: 1. Working with numbers 2. Thinking deeply to solve problems
Your skills: 1. 2. 3. 4. 5.	Other people: 1. 2. 3. 4. 5.	Your preferences: 1. 2. 3. 4. 5.

BRAND 'ME'

If you were a type of breakfast cereal what would you be? Something fun, sugary and made in a crazy shape perhaps? Or something that is sugar-free and healthy? We can't be both things at once though – people need clarity when making a purchase decision. When we think about creating opportunities and the conversations we will have with people when networking it's helpful to know what our brand is and to communicate a consistent brand message. We need to be congruent, which means that what we say and do supports our perceived brand. For example, if we're telling someone that we're a highly detail-conscious person and then catch them looking down at our muddy shoes, we'll know that we're sending out mixed messages. A classic mistake is to tell someone that we're a good listener… and then continue to tell them about a friend who was a poor listener and wouldn't stay quiet! What we do, how we speak, how we act and how we dress all help to confirm or undermine someone else's perception of us.

What is your brand? How would your friends describe you in three words? Have a look at the table below and circle *three* words that best describe you:

3-WORD BRAND

Expert	Diligent	Practical	Punctual
Numerate	Confident	Articulate	Adaptable
Accommodating	Resilient	Driven	Caring
Ethical	Tough	Skilled	Polite
Personable	Proactive	Friendly	Reliable
Resourceful	Smart	Playful	Assertive
Incisive	Creative	Outgoing	Empathetic

MY PERSONAL BRAND IN THREE WORDS IS:		

Now that we have a clearer sense of brand values we can use them to differentiate ourselves, because it is unlikely that others will have the same skills and work preferences *and* use the same words to describe their own brand. We can weave our brand words into our introduction to others and add them to our business card and internet profiles to keep the message consistent.

Differentiation is a vital aspect of creating opportunities because it enables people to make a positive choice. We hope they will choose us, which they will if we closely fit their need and they can tell us apart from a near competitor. But be careful if you're trying to hedge your bets by choosing six words, on the basis that you really can't choose only three – more words can bring less clarity and instead make us sound *indecisive*.

If you're struggling to choose a concise brand description share your thoughts with a friend and see if they can help you to focus, because if you can't choose and be clear about yourself, then it's unlikely that a potential customer will be able to either.

HOW TO RECOGNISE AN OPPORTUNITY

Anything that makes our heart beat faster, catches our eye or makes us pause momentarily in our conversation is an opportunity. Recognising this is often about allowing our intuition to pop up and say: '*Hello, I like that.*' We can trust our senses to alert us to things that we like and notice when we are taking extra care over something. We might not be able to articulate what it is exactly that has grabbed our attention – the skill is to catch ourselves in the moment, to pause and consider where we are and what is happening.

HOW TO RECOGNISE IF IT'S RIGHT FOR ME

Once we have spotted an opportunity it is good practice to weigh it against our current activities and longer-term directions. If we flip back to the first chapter, we can see if this opportunity is in line with the goals that we listed. We can also see if it fits with our skills and preferred working styles that we wrote down a few pages ago. If the opportunity falls outside all of these then we need to be cautious as we may be convincing ourselves to take an opportunity on a knee-jerk basis. If in doubt, we can sleep on it and see how we feel in the morning, because our brain will have had time to digest and analyse the information in the night.

CASE STUDY – JANET

Janet was asked by Leslie if she would like to purchase his payroll consultancy business, which advised on suitable pay grades and remuneration structures for local authority organisations. Although Janet was flattered to be asked and initially showed a strong interest because it overlapped with her organisational development work, her interest soon waned when she took a closer look at the business. There were three problems that caused her concern:

- She didn't have any experience in that industry and therefore felt she had a credibility issue with the clients.
- The actual work was repetitive and contained more numerical activities than she really liked.
- The day rate for the work was relatively low and although the work was regular, the scope for increasing the fee was limited.

Janet politely thanked Leslie for his interest and declined the opportunity – largely because the work content was not to her liking. Choosing a job because it has large rewards can be counter-productive if we're bored with the work and struggle to motivate ourselves.

HOW TO ACT ON IT

If we spot an opportunity we need to make a note of it and promptly follow up on it.[20] We can ask for another meeting to explore things further, or we can send an email to register our interest and ask for more information. If the opportunity is 'hot' and needs prompt action then it can pay to call the person concerned, rather than waiting for them to reply to an email. Telephone calls are active, whereas emailing can be more passive and we don't want to be forgotten. Be prepared to find diary space at short notice – which might mean rescheduling existing commitments, if you think this new opportunity justifies the risk of upsetting people who have already inked you into their diary.

SPOTTING MARKET TRENDS

It is important when we're foraging for opportunities to keep asking people:

> What has changed in the market?

If we keep pace with changes we can discard old opportunities that are no longer relevant and embrace new ones that will bring us more success. An example of this concerns the book industry itself where, until fairly recently, ebooks were the preserve of the amateur self-publishing author. However, once the tablet market

---

[20] Writing things down is more reliable than relying on our memory, which is liable to be under stress and apt to forget important points of interest.

exploded, following the introduction of the iPad and other similar products, people suddenly wanted ebooks to read. Publishers will now routinely print paper copies and code an ebook at the same time, but just two years ago they were mostly focussed on paper books. If someone offered you the chance to buy a book printing business now, would you?

WE CAN STAY SAFE AND STILL GROW

When considering opportunities it's reassuring to know that we don't need to have *all* the skills to take advantage of a new business option – we can work out what training we need and find ways to gain experience. Similarly, if we have a *confidence-gap* between what we'd like to do and what we think we can do, it's possible to stay safe and take small steps – I gave myself an easy entry into coaching by starting with my colleagues at work. If we're looking at a franchise opportunity many of them will come bundled with a training package and ongoing follow-up support... and if they don't, we need to be asking why not.

If we know someone who is already working in a field that we'd like to move into we can ask to shadow them and get a feel for things before committing ourselves. Also, when we first find an opportunity there can be a momentary scare as we weigh the desire to take advantage of it against the worry that we might not be able to make it work. This often happens when we first read a job description and notice where we fit the role requirements and where there are gaps. This is perfectly natural and is our way of exercising caution. We can embrace the fear and think about what it's telling us – perhaps the message is that this is a good opportunity and we need to explore the risks in a methodical manner.

SUMMARY & NEW HABIT #11

Summary

Opportunities are everywhere and there are always more available than we might think. By chatting with people, listening to them and connecting their needs and ideas to our own goals we can learn to notice new opportunities. The internet is a good place to start, but we need to remember that opportunities are often generated in relaxed face-to-face conversation, where the relationship can grow and develop. A good rule to follow is that the more people we meet, the more opportunities we will create for ourselves.

OUR NEW HABIT TO HELP US BOUNCE BACK:

- Become adept at noticing when our intuition spots an opportunity, so that we can act on it promptly.

Sales Secrets

– Method matters –

SELLING IS ESSENTIAL

Mention the need to *sell* themselves or their products and confident people turn to jelly and assertive managers curl up and shiver at the thought. However, if we don't embrace the need to sell then we really are going to have problems bouncing back, because nobody is going to be buying anything from us. We don't have to be the world's best salesperson in order to succeed – we just need to do well enough to secure our next job or customer. If we stick to sensible methods and learn from the secrets listed below then we can make a tangible difference to help us bounce back.

SELLING CONFIDENCE

We need to try out our own products or services before we can sell them, because we need to believe in them so we can talk about them with calm authority. If we worked in a café we'd expect to taste the food to make sure it was up to standard and to provide customers with a personal recommendation of what to have for lunch. If we're a landscape gardener we could first try out a piece of equipment in our garden, if we sell personality profiles we can get our own report before working with our first client, and if we're a hotelier we need to spend a night in the worst bedroom in our own hotel. (So that we find out what it's like for the people who can't afford the best room – and if we don't want to sleep in the worst room, how can we possibly charge money for it?)

If we have to demonstrate a product we need to practice hard so that we give a flawless performance on the day and convince the customer that it is the product for them. A friend of mine would practice assembling and disassembling their special packing case at least three times while simultaneously describing the product and answering predictable, but imaginary, questions. His colleagues laughed at him as he repeated the work until he was 'note perfect', but they stopped laughing when he returned to the factory the next day with an order worth more than £100,000.

If we're not feeling confident about selling then we need to know our products and we also need to know *ourselves* – because people buy people. We need to know what we like about the product or service, why we would buy it, what features and benefits it has that appeal to us and how it adds value to our lives. The same holds true if we're the product and we're going for a job interview – if we don't know our CV well enough we could struggle to provide the interviewers with adequate answers.

Finally, when we're actually out selling to people, we need to remember that:

- Without anybody selling anything to anyone the world order would collapse.
- We have a right to try and sell good things to good people.
- We can sell great products and services that we believe in.

- We can learn what to do and how to do it (because salespeople are not born – they're made).
- We can be nervous and still excel at the same time.
- We all need to value our time and our products and services.
- We all need to value our skills and strengths.
- We can be a competent salesperson and that's good enough.

SECRETS OF SUCCESS #1

\>> **Listen**. People buy from people – which means they are more likely to buy something from people who are polite, make their case clearly and who engage them in conversation. In particular, they will warm to people who listen to them. Our first secret of success is that selling is not about talking, it's about *listening*.

When we are listened to we feel good about ourselves and as a result feel positively towards the other person, which means we are more likely to buy from them. If we listen to a potential client we can understand what they like or dislike and what they really need. Listening allows us to respond appropriately to the other person and it gives us time to think of our answer rather than making snap comments.

If you can listen, you can sell.

- What can you do to become a more effective listener? Take notes? Switch off your phone? Maintain better eye contact?

SECRETS OF SUCCESS #2

\>> **Turn a hard sell into an easy buy**. People often talk about the 'hard sell' where the client is bombarded with facts and arguments to convince them to make a purchase, leaving them with little room for doubt – Product 'A' really *is* the one to go for because it is obviously the best product! However, we don't really like to be sold to in this way, and as consumers become more sophisticated they are more likely to resist a hard sell and walk away from the deal. Therefore, we need to turn a hard sell into an easy buy – we need to make it so the other person finds it easy to say 'yes'.

An example of this is a handyman offering to tidy up our garden for £100. We might want the work done, but feel uncomfortable spending that amount of money on someone we don't really know. He pushes harder and explains all the great things he can do, but we feel put under pressure and aren't really convinced. Then he changes tack and says that as an introductory offer he will do two hours' work for £20 so we can see how good he is. Suddenly we agree, because £20 is much easier to say yes to and our hunch is that in two hours he can sort out 70% of the mess anyway. He knows that if we get to know him we are more likely to spend the £100 on another occasion. He has turned a hard sell into an easy buy.

- What can you do to make your products or services easy to say yes to? Have an introductory offer? Change your price points? Develop a low cost entry-level product?[21]

SECRET OF SUCCESS #3

>> Speak to people. We can use the internet effectively to make contact with interesting and worthwhile people and we can then meet up with them to talk in person. This is because, as we've said already – people buy people. We might buy a car because the salesperson did a better job than the person at a neighbouring garage. That's why so many celebrities endorse products – we buy things from people we trust, even if we don't really know much about the item that we're buying. Our key sales task is to talk to people – the salespeople with the best performance are often the

---

[21] I had to learn this for myself when I realised that a new and more expensive coaching course wasn't selling as well as I'd hoped. So I stopped selling it and developed a cheaper 3-day course that was more cost effective for organisations. This resulted in more sales almost overnight.

ones who speak with the most people, because it's a numbers game – the more people who know us, the more we are likely to sell to.

- How many people have you spoken to in the last month? What can you do to speak to at least 20 people in the next four weeks?

SECRETS OF SUCCESS #4

>> **Maintain a ratio of 6:1.** When trying to decide how many opportunities to create for ourselves we need to be sure that we have enough at the start of our sales process so at least one will make it through to the end and become a sale or a new client, or a new job. Current market trends suggest that it is prudent to maintain a ratio of 6-to-1, meaning that for every one success we're aiming for we need to have six opportunities in play. We need to replace them as they age or fizzle out, because we never know which one will eventually come to fruition.

If we're aiming to secure a job, however, we're not looking at a ratio of six applications for one job – that would be a foolishly low number to aim for. Instead we can aim for six top-quality applications for each of the four or five first interviews that we might need before we are offered a second interview. Therefore, we need to maintain at least 30 realistic opportunities for ourselves and keep this number topped up as old applications fall by the wayside.

- How many live opportunities do you currently have for each sale or interview that you need to secure? What can you do to maintain a 6:1 ratio of opportunities to potential successes?

SECRETS OF SUCCESS #5

>> **Manage our pipeline.** If we are methodical and follow a process then we will greatly increase our chances of success – in the same way that a farmer will plough and harrow the land, plant crops, fertilise them, keep the pests away, water the green shoots and look after them until they ripen into a field of corn to be harvested. He also needs to make sure he doesn't have 'leakage' at any stage so that he plants all the seeds he buys, harvests the whole crop and makes sure the grain is all weighed and invoiced for. He will manage each stage of the process so that he maximises the return on his time and money spent. We need to do the same with our sales pipeline because it's pointless putting in effort to meet people if we never follow up with a call or an email. Here is a simple sales process:

SIX-MONTH SALES PROCESS		
To find a new client	STAGE	To find a new job[22]
Research organisations and networking groups where potential clients might be found	1	Research advertisements and cold call opportunities
Send introductory letters and visit networking group	2	Send out introductory letters and apply for roles
Follow-up call to arrange an introductory meeting	3	Follow up to show interest
Meet and find out about the other person, listen and think about how we could help them	4	Receive an invitation to a first interview or assessment centre

[22] The book *Job Hunting 3.0* goes into considerable detail about process, measurement and how to use ratios to measure performance.

Follow up with a letter and offer possible solutions	5	Follow up to thank them for seeing us
Call to arrange a second meeting	6	Invited to attend a second interview
Meet them again and talk through our 'easy buy' for them	7	Follow up to thank them again
Ask for the order	8	Be made an offer
Receive the order	9	Consider the offer
Sign and celebrate	10	Sign and celebrate

Now that we have a clear process we can measure how many opportunities there are at each stage and see if we are putting in enough at the front end. We also need to be proactive and work diligently to move opportunities through the sales pipeline, because they rarely move themselves.

SECRETS OF SUCCESS #6

>> **Mine our contacts.** Whenever we meet someone it pays to collect a business card or an email address and make sure they're all logged in our contact book, be it paper or electronic. When we need to boost our sales activities we can use a broadcast email service such as *Swiftpage, MailChimp* or *Constant Contact* to send a short letter to everyone. These services can be free to use for smaller campaigns and are a great way to get our message out. If we try and send hundreds of emails through our own system we run the risk of being tagged as a spammer, and that would be very bad news.

Our letter can be informative, detail what we are looking for and have words in *italics* or in **bold** or <u>underlined</u> to break up the flow of plain text and make key points stand out. A good tip is to aim for three or four paragraphs as people often prefer longer letters. Additional detail helps them to understand our products or services more clearly than a snappy two-line pitch does. People also need to be clearly told what we want them to do once they have read the contents, so include a call to action, such as:

- Email us now for more information!
- Forward this to someone who you think could help me!
- Click on the link to view the pictures!

These kinds of instructions do generate a response and it's possible to monitor click-through rates to see who opened our message. Also add a 'P.S.' after your sign-off – studies show that a large proportion of readers simply scan down to the Post Script at the end to see if there is a new product on offer. Bearing this in mind, we can add a line here to reinforce our central message or to promote an additional product.

SECRETS OF SUCCESS #7

>> **Track our process.** Sales success requires organisation so that we capture potential opportunities and shepherd them through a series of gates until one or more result in an invitation to an interview or the order being booked. If we don't properly file our opportunities we'll probably end up with a pile of notes stuffed into a drawer and this leaves too much to chance. This is where a *sales tracker spreadsheet* helps – we can build a simple one in Microsoft Excel (or in Numbers for Macs) to reflect the potential customers we are currently engaged with and the stage of the process they are at. Here is an example for a fictional business:

SALES TRACKER FOR BISHOP'S BULK BUILDING SUPPLIES LTD

Client	Opportunity	Pipeline Stage	Action Date	Action Task
Hewitt Ltd	Nails £500	3	Jan	Arrange 1st meeting
Daniels LLP	Scaffolding £2,500	3	Feb	Arrange 1st meeting
Merritt Co	Safety hats £750	5	Jan	Email options
Holmes Corp	Paint £450	6	Mar	Arrange 2nd meeting
Forrest Partners	Screws £300	3	Feb	Arrange 1st meeting
King Plc	Wood £6,000	7/8	Jan	Deliver presentation
Todd & Sons	Hammers £100	2	Feb	Send brochure

The tracker shows the essential information for each opportunity we have and we can easily sort the columns by action dates to keep current tasks in sight. At the end of each month we need to update the tracker, revise the action dates to reflect our progress and re-sort it again to show what our priority actions are for the next month. In time, our spreadsheet may contain 50 or more opportunities but we only need to be working on those that require attention this month, making life manageable for us.

If we keep good records and follow a sales process the two become mutually supportive and will improve our chances of success. However, if we want to live dangerously we can always stick with scraps of paper in a drawer and a random fling-mud-at-the-wall-and-hope-some-sticks process.

The choice is yours: *Which course will you choose?*

SECRET OF SUCCESS #8

>> **Have tiered products.** One way to create opportunities for an easy buy is to have a range of products that enables people to make purchases at a price point that works for them. In our local town there is a gallery selling original pieces of art and they have designed their range to be affordable to a wide cross section of tourists – from people who have only £10 to spend, up to those who might commission a piece of work for £500. This strategy has enabled them to thrive in a very competitive environment because their affordable art is an easy buy for many people.

SECRETS OF SUCCESS #9

>> **Ask for the order.** We can make a great pitch and think the sell is going well, but if we don't actually *ask* for the order and seal the deal then we can let money slip through our hands. Remember: if we're good enough to deliver the work then we're good enough to ask for it! And we can ask for the money too at the end of the piece. Here are a few ways we can ask for the order:

- Can you confirm the order please?
- Can you send me a purchase order?
- Shall we get our diaries out, book in a date and then I will email you a confirmation?
- This is how I earn my living, so I would like to value my time here. Preferably I'd like to charge £50 for my time, payable by cheque. Would both of these things be ok?

- When would like you like to book in for, Monday afternoon or Tuesday morning?
- I would like to pause the conversation, before we go on, and confirm that you're ok to proceed with the business terms we previously discussed?
- Here are our standard terms of business. If I fill in the details now (writes on form)… can you sign here please to indicate acceptance?

Remember to thank your clients for their business. Sometimes I give clients extra time, free workshops or a free book as a goodwill offering and often a simple 'thank you' is enough and goes a long way. We all liked to be thanked and as we're getting paid for the work, we have a lot to be thankful for!

SECRETS OF SUCCESS #10

>> Keep going. It can take three years to build a business – one year to make a loss, two years to break even and three years to make a profit. It can take six to twelve months to find a new job. It can take six browsers in a shop to get one who will buy a product. What this means is that we have to plan our life to account for these timescales. We can't lose heart if we start work on Monday and haven't sold anything by Friday, because bouncing back requires continual effort. The secret of success for most people is that *they kept going* through bad times and rainy days until they succeeded.

CASE STUDY – PHILIP

Philip was an experienced builder working for a firm of contractors who specialised in building large factories and office spaces.

Although a brick layer by trade, he could turn his hand to most things and when his job was made redundant, he decided to set up a sole trader business as a local builder and handyman specialising in small projects. Although he wasn't used to selling his expertise on the open market he started by joining a networking club, which he found nerve-wracking at first. However, it gave him the confidence to stand up in front of people and talk about his work, which started to create a steady stream of small orders: building walls, re-pointing brickwork, clearing gutters, repairing storm damage and so on.

In order to find more work he set up a spreadsheet of all the people he knew and every six weeks he used a mail system to send out a short letter with content geared to seasonal activity. Writing to established contacts can have a much higher success rate than cold calling and he noticed that this approach brought him more work. He also developed the habit of always leaving two business cards with each client – one for them *and* another to hand on to a friend or neighbour. Over time this tactic also generated useful referral work.

When I spoke to him about his sales technique his view was that a little of everything meant that he covered several routes to market himself. He couldn't know in advance which one would be the most productive, so it made sense to broaden his approach. It took him ten months to secure enough work for his business to become sustainable, but then it continued at a pace he was comfortable with until he elected to retire.

SUMMARY & NEW HABIT #12

Summary

We are all good people and can all excel at selling. We can also banish any self-limiting stereotypes we might think about because they're unhelpful and likely to undermine our confidence. Whether we're looking for a job or building our business, it doesn't matter if we experience a setback: our skills and talents are still intact. By bearing in mind the secrets of success we can do well for ourselves – there is no special magic to winning new business, only *thoughtful, determined application.*

Secrets of Sales Success

1. Listen
2. Turn a hard sell into an easy buy
3. Speak to people
4. Maintain a ratio of 6:1
5. Manage our pipeline
6. Mine our contacts
7. Track our process
8. Have tiered products
9. Ask for the order
10. Keep going

OUR NEW HABIT TO HELP US BOUNCE BACK:

- Keep talking to people about our products or services, so that our sales pipeline remains topped up and opportunities for new business continue to flow through.

Embracing Social Media

– Free, fun and useful –

BE IN THE GAME

If you think social media is just a giant chat room full of people with too much time on their hands, then think again – the business world is increasingly shifting across to social media platforms. So much so that a leading international consultancy organisation recently declared that they would cease using email for internal communications within 18 months. Their forward-thinking view is that social media is faster, reduces the workload and removes the need to maintain an expensive and complicated in-house server system.[23] Social media is here to stay and we have to choose how to embrace it and where to focus our efforts. If we're part of a wide expanse of networks we can make new friends and create new opportunities.

A couple of my business colleagues shudder whenever I mention social media activities and we laugh that, as long as I'm doing the work for them, they don't have to sully their hands with it. They might not need it right now, perhaps because they have

---

[23] The company is Atos and they have already reported a 20% drop in email traffic, replaced by the use of Facebook chat, MSN and other social media applications. Sources: www.huffingtonpost.co.uk and www.geekosystem.com

full order books or feel that it isn't good business for them, but what do you think they'll do if one day the work starts to dry up?

Social media is a wide and complex topic so in this chapter we will focus on why it's so useful, encourage people to think about the various platforms on offer and then zoom in on one that is worth serious consideration – *Twitter*.

A SHOCK

My own interest in social media started when I visited a potential client with a colleague and our meeting began with the client asking us how we sold our training packages. He smiled and asked if we:

- Use Facebook adverts? *No.*
- Use Google adverts? *No.*
- Write a blog? *No.*
- Use Twitter? *No.*
- Have a Facebook fan page? *No.*
- Send out emails via LinkedIn? *No.*
- Join in a discussion on any LinkedIn groups? *No.*
- Take advantage of any other platforms? *Errr… No.*

He was incredulous and wanted to know:

'What did we do?'

'We visit people,' my colleague said sincerely, like a man who knows a thing or two about selling.

'Is that it?' Our potential customer replied, arching an eyebrow.

'Wow!' He added, amazed that there were still people who didn't surf the rolling waves of social media interaction. He was too polite to actually *call* us dinosaurs, but the surprised look on his face clearly suggested that we were heading for fossilisation in the near future. The experience was chastening and I realised that if our prospective client was operating confidently in the social media space then we had to be there too.

> ## TOP TIP
> Go where your clients live.
> If they live in the social media space then we need to as well,
> or we could easily lose out to a competitor.

CHOOSE YOUR PLATFORMS

There are several competing social media platforms and there's nothing wrong in trying them all and finding out what works for you and your business. In my experience the differences between them are increasingly blurred as they each try to capture lucrative advertising income and paid-for networking services. However, we have to remember that *we* are the product that's being sold. The immense databases that these websites generate are their most valuable asset and this information is packaged, sliced and sold to generate more advertising revenue.

The three major platforms in the UK are *LinkedIn, Facebook* and *Twitter*. They are now joined by *Pinterest, Google+, Bebo, MySpace, Vimeo, Ning, Orkut* and *Flickr*. They all have value, but for me, spending more time on fewer sites is better than trying to cover all the options and spreading my effort too thin. I use LinkedIn and Facebook and have found that Twitter gave me the best results when I needed to bounce back, because it's engaging, simple and responsive.

NO DAISY CHAINS

It is possible to link up Twitter with LinkedIn and Facebook so that tweets are broadcast across all the platforms at once, saving time and increasing their usefulness. However, this can be dangerous because each site has its own subtleties and audiences. What works on Twitter can look out of place on LinkedIn, so be careful… do you want your next boss to be reading your tweets about the party you've just been to? We get one chance to make a good first impression, so it's much safer to keep the feeds on each site *separate* or we could inadvertently undermine our brand.

USING LINKEDIN

LinkedIn is great for business people and job hunters, with a comprehensive suite of special interest groups that we can join. We can take part in discussions and make new contacts from a wide variety of backgrounds. We need to make sure that our profile is up-to-date, and think about the kind of clients we want to attract and check that our profile is aligned with our goals. It's also worth asking colleagues to provide us with testimonials as they can help to establish our credibility.

USING FACEBOOK

Facebook is constantly expanding and is increasingly being used as a serious business tool. It is possible to run separate lists for family, friends and work colleagues, but I find this too much to manage and instead simply make sure that anything I post is something that I don't mind everyone knowing about. Facebook is growing in complexity, almost on a daily basis, and well worth exploring. We can grow our network through useful 'fan pages' (now called 'Facebook Business Pages') that invite people to 'like' them. These pages are almost a mini website to which we can stream blog content, links and comments. There are also targeted advertising opportunities which could work well for our business, although we need to add any planned expenditure to our cash flow forecast and consider the impact of such. As a general rule, advertising always costs more than we think it will and takes longer for its value to be realised.

USING TWITTER

When I wanted to bounce back I realised that part of the problem was that I only knew a few local people, because most of my work to-date had been across the UK and not close to home. I decided to change this, having previously found that networking locally saves time and money, is easy to do and can be more productive than travelling far and wide to meet new people. Twitter allows you to 'follow' anyone, which means that it's easy to search for people in our area and begin a conversation, because we can use our geographic proximity as a point of commonality. While Facebook and LinkedIn require the other person to accept our invitation, Twitter only requires this for locked accounts.[24] People may decide to follow us back and a few may not, but it's this ease of access to people that is Twitter's great strength.

The other strength is its simplicity – you have a maximum of 140 characters to compose your message, which encourages people to get straight to the point or to have fun writing pithy or humorous messages. Twitter also has an immediacy that people find appealing, and *tweeters* (messages are known as *tweets* and people who send them are called *tweeters*) often have a Twitter application open on their desktop or smartphone and browse it regularly throughout the day.[25] It's a fast and efficient route to market ourselves, costs nothing to use and is a great way to meet people, stay in touch with clients and sell our products and services.

Twitter also enables us to get to know clients outside of work.

[24] Locked accounts are for people who wish to remain private. If we're building our network for business then we should keep our account unlocked as it makes us easier to follow and builds contacts more quickly.
[25] Take a look at *Tweetdeck*, *Hootsuite* and *Ubersocial* – there are lots of other apps as well.

This can seem a little odd at first because it blurs the boundaries between work and life, but it's a good way to make deeper friendships that can spill over into longer lasting business.

GETTING STARTED ON TWITTER

Some people are wary of getting started on Twitter because they have a false assumption that the conversations are 'boring drivel'. However, human interaction is comprised of all sorts of discussions ranging from the intense to the frivolous, and new contacts often need to 'warm up' to us by having simple conversations that are easy and safe.

Twitter can take us out into the world – instead of being a lone person slogging away in a study trying to find a job or build a business, we can be connected to hundreds of people at once. This is good for our morale and helps keep us motivated. I've found that tweeting a simple message such as 'I'm making toast for breakfast, who wants jam and who wants marmalade?' can start fun conversations with people and let us begin the day with a smile. These simple chats make us an easy person to get to know, which results in us making more friends and perhaps talking with them at a deeper level on other occasions. Twitter allows us to operate at our own pace and depth and to join in other conversations as and when we feel confident to do so. Here are 10 top tips to get started:

> **TOP TEN TWITTER TIPS**
> Getting Started
> 1. **Give yourself a catchy name** – we can have a name that says something about us and which doesn't reveal our true identity, if that makes us feel more comfortable.[26]

---

[26] My twitter name is @RichardMaun because I'm my own brand name. Do say hello on Twitter and I will follow you back.

2. **Use a smiley photo of ourselves** – people like people and a photograph helps others to connect better with us.

3. **If our account is for business then leave it unlocked** – this makes it easier for others to follow us.

4. **If our account is for personal networking we might decide to lock it** – if we want private conversations, or feel nervous about starting out, we can lock our account to begin with. Locking it requires us to accept people before they can follow us and read our comments.

5. **Follow a mixture of men and women** – we can't tell who will be chatty and friendly. Part of the joy of Twitter is meeting people who we wouldn't normally bump into in our daily life.

6. **Don't moan too much** – if all we do is grumble then people will soon get fed up, just like they do in real life! One of them could be a potential client.

7. **Don't retweet too much** – a retweeted message broadcasts a tweet back to our followers and is a good way to share interesting comments. However, too many retweets can look a bit lazy and can frustrate people as they want to know about us and not just the people whose comments we are sharing.

8. **Start by going on at different times of the day** – this will help us to get an idea of who is chatting and when they tend to be active, as people come and go throughout the day. Meal times are a good opportunity to dip into the timelines because that's when our friends will tend to take a break from work and say hello to us.

9. **Don't just trust anyone** – as is the case with real life, we need to exercise reasonable caution with other people online until we get to know them better. We can read people's blogs, visit their websites and see whom they talk to and what they say as part of the process of building trust. Despite the 140-character limit, our personality is evident in our tweets and we can get a feel of what a person is like from their posts.

10. **Beware of spam** – if you get an unsolicited direct message (called a DM) selling something, for example, then it's good practice to *block* the person who sent it. It's worth knowing that sometimes an account may get hacked, you may be spammed, or a naughty tweeter might overstep the mark. When these things happen (assume they will at some point), deal with it swiftly and move on. Some people feel that it's wrong to block people and lack the confidence to do so. The facility is there to keep us safe from silliness or abuse and not using it merely makes it easier for troublemakers to cause a nuisance to ourselves and our friends.

Getting started on Twitter is no different to us arriving in a large city. We need to keep our wits about us, steer clear of shady alleys and trouble spots and make sure our wallet remains out of sight. Start by setting yourself a small target, such as to follow five people from your local area and to say hello to them over the course of a week. Once we have a sense of how it works we can build our followers quite quickly by systematically following people, who will generally follow us back, because that is the etiquette on Twitter.

WHAT TO SAY ON TWITTER

If the thought of saying hello and actually tweeting seems like an easy thing to suggest and a tough challenge in real life, here are 10 more tips to get you started:

TOP TEN TWITTER TIPS

How to Tweet

1. **Say hello and ask people how their day is going** – this is an easy question to answer. Recently I tweeted just 'Hello 😊' to 10 people whom I hadn't chatted with for a while and went on to have lots of fun conversations with them. Sometimes we have to make the first move!

2. **Ask a specific question** – such as if people are going to watch a particular television programme or what they think about a film or a news item.

3. **Ask for help** – Twitter is a fantastic source of knowledge and asking for help with a problem, or canvassing opinion when deciding what to buy, can yield many helpful and constructive replies.

4. **Tell people what you're doing** – we all do mundane things and it's comforting to know we're not the only one doing them, so it is okay to say what you're up to. For example, people might tweet out 'I'm bored of work – aargh!' Or perhaps 'Had fun planting some flowers.'

5. **Respond to comments about TV shows** – Twitter can be hilarious when people watch a television programme and tweet at the same time, so join in the fun and make new friends.

6. **Tweet a picture** – if you go for a walk perhaps and there is a fetching landscape, take a photograph and post it to the timeline. People often respond with a comment – for example, when I tweet a picture of our local beach I'll get people replying that they wish they were there too!

7. **Talk about your hobby** – many people often talk about their favourite football team, for example, and follow fellow supporters as their shared interest makes it easy for them to chat.

8. **'Make' toast** – I've said this before, but people find 'silly' questions fun and engaging – you can have a laugh and make friends by pretending to give them a slice of toast with their choice of topping. I've started fun conversations simply by tweeting 'Having toast for breakfast… who would like a slice?' Or 'what shall I have to eat for lunch?'

9. **Use *hashtags*** – these are a way of flagging a tweet with the # symbol. People use them to make their tweet easier to find, to be ironic or to denote a series of tweets. For example, you could tweet about film titles that contain a colour and use a hashtag to tell people it's a fun series of tweets, such as: *The Colour Purple #filmswithcoloursinthetitle*. Or *The Woman in Black #filmswithcoloursinthetitle*. Other people will then reply with their own suggestions and use your hashtag to show that they're playing along with you. People are very inventive with hashtags, so feel free to join in the fun!

10. **Respond to other tweets** – comment on what your friends are saying, offer support, ask them questions or just be a friend to them.

There is one golden rule on Twitter: *No drunk tweeting.* Once people have had a few drinks they lose their focus and can tweet all sorts of things that they regret in the morning. The same goes for expressing controversial opinions – if you position yourself as a polite and caring person and then one day are fed up and tweet a lot of abusive comments, you will destroy a large chunk of your brand credibility. Twitter works both ways – if we are friendly we make friends, but if we are divisive, sexist, racist or just plain obnoxious then we will lose friends quickly.

USING TWITTER TO SELL

In terms of bouncing back, Twitter is a great platform to sell things from because it is interactive and people will click on a link if it interests them. The Twitter timeline can be like a giant scrolling shop window – there are always new things waiting to be discovered. For example, a few of the people in my timeline sell children's clothes and one of them posted a photo of a superhero cape that she had made for a friend. I tweeted her and asked to buy two capes for my children, not knowing that the one in the picture was just a one-off. She agreed to make the capes and then, realising there was a market for capes for small boys, added them to her online shop as a permanent product. Twitter works because people feel that they know you, like you and therefore are more likely to take a look at a product or service you're selling – unlike cold calling, where people tend to put the phone down or walk away.

We can use twitter to boost our sales and create new opportunities by:

- Inviting people to read our blog.
- Inviting people to visit our LinkedIn profile.
- Inviting people to visit our Facebook fan page.

- Inviting people for a 'tweetup', where you meet for a coffee and a chat. This is a good way to cement friendships or get to know possible clients.
- Publicising our business website.
- Advertising specific products or events, with a link to a website for more information.
- Telling people what we do and inviting them to contact us.
- Using scheduled tweets to make sure that our interesting invitations or links appear in the timeline at specific points in the day.
- Using a third-party app such as Hootsuite or Tweetdeck to manage our Twitter account and create lists of potential customers. We can say hello to these people and draw their attention to a product or service.

MAINTAINING OUR NETWORKS

Whichever social media platform we use to engage with people, we need to allow time for maintenance and upkeep as each site is constantly being upgraded. Simply setting up a LinkedIn account doesn't count as engaging with social media – we need to allocate time to make sure our biographies are up-to-date and reflect on what we're currently trying to achieve. We also need to spend time talking to people and being an active participant on the sites.

CASE STUDY – RICHARD

At the beginning of the book I talked about how I had made social media a key part of my *bouncing back* strategy, so it seems appropriate to end the book by reflecting on my experiences. At the outset I set targets for the number of LinkedIn and Facebook followers I wanted and made sure I reached them. I also decided that learning to use Twitter was essential because of its simplicity and the fact that it could help me to quickly build a local network of contacts. LinkedIn and Facebook have been useful in reaching those people not on Twitter, but Twitter has been by far and away the most effective tool for me. I ran Facebook advert campaigns, but they didn't work for me, and I found them expensive to maintain. The same applies to Google ads, which were good for generating interest in my website, but not so good for converting people into clients. Your story will be different and if we try several options we will find what works the best for us. Here's how I have benefitted from Twitter:

- ✓ One of my largest clients was introduced to me by a Twitter contact who read my blog and liked the kind of work that I could do.
- ✓ My publisher has increasingly looked at the size of my network when considering new book contracts, because it shows them that I have a large personal market to sell to.
- ✓ When I needed to employ a *centre manager* as part of my business accreditation project, I used Twitter to find someone local who could do the job. Interestingly, the person I hired wasn't on Twitter, but their friend was and she put the two of us in contact.
- ✓ I have sold books via Twitter, by tweeting the link to the relevant Amazon.co.uk page.
- ✓ I have built up the readership of my weekly *modern careers* blog by adding comments to Facebook, LinkedIn and Twitter so people know it exists and they can click through and read my latest post at www.richardmaun.com
- ✓ I have deepened a few client relationships by enjoying social conversations with people outside of work.

✓ We tweet the details of our radio show each week and that has helped us to attract listeners from around the UK, America, Canada, Germany, Australia, Norway and Singapore. Check out www.futureradio.co.uk/businesslife for show podcasts.

✓ Through Twitter, I've made new business friends whom I've networked with and met up for coffee and cake. These people have given me ideas for business, introduced me to new clients and been a useful source of advice and encouragement.

When I started my journey I had just a few Facebook friends and LinkedIn contacts. I didn't know anything about Twitter, or have a blog or a new book to sell, or need a centre manager, or know who might be a good local client to aim for. I knew less than 20 people locally whom I could have telephoned and met up with as part of my networking activities. Within a month of starting to use Twitter that number grew to 200 and now I'm linked to over 2,000 people across the UK. I've invested my time to good effect and have worked hard to make it work for me. Social media is there to connect us to the world and if we want to bounce back then time invested in this area can bring handsome rewards.

SUMMARY & NEW HABIT #13

Summary

When we're in the process of bouncing back, social media is a good way of finding new people to interact with and it enables us to travel round the world and create new opportunities for ourselves without having to leave our chair. By spending time on platforms that are relevant to us we can find new opportunities to market ourselves and expose our products and services to a wider audience. If we're looking for a job we can increase the size and reach of our networks and talk to people who might know someone who needs our skills. If we have a fear about using social media, we can take positive steps to keep ourselves safe, learn from people whom we trust and follow their advice. Social media is here to stay and once we overcome our natural shyness and join in conversations we will help ourselves to bounce back.

OUR NEW HABIT TO HELP US TO BOUNCE BACK:

- Choose a major social media platform and spend some time in that space every day. We can increase our network, talk to people, share thoughts and ideas, have fun and explore all the related services on offer.

Make a Change
– Learn to keep learning –

THE NEED TO LEARN

None of us have been in this exact situation before, and we will need to learn something new in order to survive and thrive. After you put this book down, make new choices to enable you to bounce back and, at the very least, make a commitment to yourself to keep learning. We're great people, we deserve to make our lives the best they can be and continuous learning is what will make a lasting difference.

7 KEY QUOTES ON LEARNING

Here are seven useful quotes to support our ongoing learning journey. Which ones will you take to heart?

> **1.** We can choose whether to stay stuck or to bounce back.

> **2.** We need to keep learning in order to bounce back.

3. If we learn nothing new, we won't know what to change.

4. If we change nothing, we will get nowhere.

5. We need to apply our learning to practical action.

6. When we make a change, we move a step forward.

7. Each new step is worth celebrating.

REMEMBER...

BOUNCING BACK
... is about creating a new world for ourselves
that brings us enough personal satisfaction to feel that we
have truly moved on from the past.

We can survive and thrive again!

THREE RULES FOR SUCCESS

If you're wondering how to bounce back successfully, or are currently stuck in the process of doing so and are pondering the way forward – whether you're looking for work, striving to build your business or making personal changes in your life – here are three simple rules for the path to success:

RULE 1
Create your own opportunities

RULE 2
Trust your intuition

RULE 3
Keep going

KEEP GOING

This book is here to support us and we can dip into it when we need to. It's full of useful tools and approaches designed to help us to do feelings, think clearly and transform ideas into practical actions. Above all else, we need to keep going – whether by increasing the flow of our physis, filling our diary with interesting appointments, using social media platforms to increase our network, or by asking a trusted friend to listen to our plans and ideas. We can be resourceful and create opportunities, because despite the limitations that appear to hedge us in, there are always options available to us.

If we keep going, life will improve and we *will* bounce back.

WELL DONE – you've reached the end of the book. You can now keep going and you can bounce back, because you're a decent, worthwhile individual with a right to be here and a right to work.

GO FOR IT!

SUMMARY & NEW HABIT #14

Summary

Never stop learning and always remember to keep going.

OUR NEW HABIT TO HELP US BOUNCE BACK:

- Keep learning something new each week so that we keep on making changes to our world, and in doing so, continue to take safe steps forward.

Tool Kit
– The essence of bouncing back –

THE ESSENTIAL HIGHLIGHTS

Here is a summary of the key tools and models featured in this book. For more detailed explanations and case studies, please refer to the original chapters. Feel free to write in answers when prompted and use this section as your space to be creative and reflective.

SECTION 1
CONTEXT & QUICK STARTS

Chapter 1 – Bouncing Back For Real

THINGS TO THINK ABOUT

- Success is often based on taking note of what is already working well and by replicating it.
- We can borrow from others in order to make life easier for ourselves.
- When bouncing back, my motto was: **Do more of what people want!** (Because you never know where it will lead.)

- We begin to bounce back when we embrace the uncomfortable truth and then create space to invite in the new. (Until that point, we're just playing at bouncing back.)

> **BOUNCING BACK...**
> ... is about creating a new world for ourselves that brings us enough satisfaction to feel that we have truly moved on from the past.
>
> We have survived and are once again thriving!

PERSONAL GOALS

Have a look at the following prompts and work out a few goals for yourself:

- Work location / Work content / Work amount / Work direction
- Home life / Fun time / Personal growth
- New skills / New horizons / Cherished ambitions

Think about your working life last week or last month and how it might be different next year... then fill in the tables below:

Last week / Last month my working life contained these things:	In the future it could have these things in it:
1)	1)
2)	2)
3)	3)
4)	4)
5)	5)

WHAT HAVE I LEARNT?

These are my learning points from my journey:

- We need to choose to bounce back instead of choosing to stay stuck – because everything flows from this decision.
- Money isn't everything.
- When life hits a trough, taking time off is a smart move.
- Having fun makes for a more productive week.
- The more we talk to people about the reality of our situation the more help and support we receive.
- Meeting new people leads to new opportunities.
- Lots of opportunities create lots of interesting ways to bounce back.
- Big progress can require big changes.

Chapter 2 – Modern Careers

> The responsibility for our modern career
> is ours and ours alone.

7 TENETS OF A MODERN CAREER

1. Not knowing exactly where we will be by retirement.
2. Not knowing when retirement will be.
3. Being able to re-train if we need to.
4. Being able to work in a variety of ways, such as an employee, a consultant or in our own start-up business.
5. Being responsible for our own money management as pension rights are increasingly eroded, we have periods out of work, or wish to self-finance a change of direction in life or work.

6. Having job-hunting skills. In my experience the UK's favourite sport isn't football or fishing – it's having an amateur hack at getting a job by trusting to luck.

7. Knowing our own skills. We need to have a good sense of what we like to do, what we are good at and how we add value. These may emerge over time in response to experience.

MODERN CAREER SKILLS – NO. 1 SPECIALIST SKILLS

These are the direct work-related skills that we have been trained in. These skills are particular to our role or industry and can include:

1. Technical language
2. Trade skills
3. Craft skills
4. Process skills

MODERN CAREER SKILLS – NO. 2 EXTERNAL SKILLS

These skills are the ones that others can see us using.

1. Productivity
2. People Skills
3. Public Relations

MODERN CAREER SKILLS – NO. 3 INTERNAL SKILLS

These are the skills that we carry with us but are not visible.

1. Agility
2. Determination
3. Humility

4. Learning
5. Reliability
6. Resilience
7. Thinking

SELF-CHECK ON LEARNING

QUESTION 1: What have I learnt over the last three years? My answer is:	QUESTION 2: How have I developed? My answer is:

WHERE ARE WE GOING NEXT?

- Find another full time role
- Look for consultancy work
- Set up as a sole-trader offering products or services
- Buy-in to an existing company
- Work in partnership with a colleague

IDENTITY & STORIES

Our identity is key to our sense of well-being. What stories do you tell about yourself?

- Our job was made redundant, not us as people.
- We can proactively make the difficult decision to close our business, instead of watching it slide away from us.
- We can choose to set up our own business, instead of telling people that we've been thrown on the scrap heap.

Chapter 3 – The Gyroscope

Our sense of self-esteem is about being confident, talented and thoughtful. We belong in the world and have a right to a decent life. We are as good as the next person and although we may have had different experiences in life other people are not better than us, or vice versa. It is our right to work and this not diminished by our age, sex, race, colour, creed, religion or family situation. We are important because we count as talented, lovable human beings.

SELF-ESTEEM STARTS HERE	
1) What skills have we retained? 1. 2. 3.	2) What qualities do we have? 1. 2. 3.
3) What else makes us employable? 1. 2. 3.	4) What compliments have we received? 1. 2. 3.
5) What is it about us that makes us a decent individual? 1. 2. 3.	

Chapter 4 – The Essence of Success

THE THREE KEY RULES FOR SUCCESS ARE:

- **Rule 1** – Create your own opportunities
- **Rule 2** – Trust your intuition
- **Rule 3** – Keep going
- **Your 4th Rule** – If you added a fourth rule for yourself, what would it be?

MY 4TH RULE IS:

_____

_____

_____

Chapter 5 – Getting Started

TOP TIPS FOR GETTING STARTED

- ✓ Stop doing things that are getting in the way
- ✓ Get up and out of bed
- ✓ Have a spring clean
- ✓ Buy a notebook
- ✓ Make a list of key supporters
- ✓ Telephone each supporter and book lunch with them

✓ Do something you really want to
✓ Do something new
✓ Volunteer
✓ Pay for professional support

TAKE SAFE STEPS FORWARDS BY:

❖ Finding the facts
❖ Being pleasantly ignorant
❖ Taking stock of equipment
❖ Practicing when you need to

SECTION 2
SKILLS & INSIGHTS FOR LONG TERM SUCCESS

Chapter 6 – The High-Cs Transition Model

1) STRESSFUL CHAOS

This is the first stage, when the 'storm' is happening now.

2) TENSE CALM

This is the second stage, when we are becalmed. After the storm passes there is nothing, just an empty waiting while we look around us.

3) FREE CLEANSING

This is the third stage, when we make a few basic changes.

4) ANXIOUS CONSIDERATION

This is the fourth stage, when we have to collect facts and draft our plans.

5) HOPEFUL CATCHING

This is the fifth stage, when we get going.

6) CAREFUL COORDINATION

This is the sixth stage, when we make progress and keep our eyes open for potential setbacks.

7) JOYFUL CELEBRATION

This is the seventh and final stage, when we reach a sustainable place and can reward ourselves.

SPOTTING INACTIVITY

Here are classic telltale signs that we are stuck and need to stop what we're doing and make new decisions:

- We find ourselves repeating patterns of behaviour in the hope that *this time* we will get a good result.
- We talk a great deal without doing anything.
- We resist practical suggestions from colleagues by peppering our answers with 'but'. For example: 'I could do that, but I don't have the time.'

- We get angry with people so they back off and leave us alone, thereby avoiding having to explain ourselves or trying new things.
- We find ourselves delaying the important work until tomorrow.
- We spend time on distractions such as polishing our desk, excessive fact-finding or giving ourselves a preparatory task that must first be completed.

Chapter 7 – Physis

SMALL WORD, BIG IMPACT

Physis (often pronounced foo-sis) means growth. In nature it's the force that ensures a tiny seed germinates and then forces its way up through a concrete paving slab. In our terms, *physis* is the force that keeps us moving forward and continuing to develop. It's the wellspring of energy and power that we all have inside us. It's part of what makes us 'us' and how we use our physis to our advantage is what makes us unique.

ACCESSING PHYSIS

It's up to us to help ourselves. Here's how:

1. Accept that we have an unlimited supply of physis.
2. Accept that we are thoughtful, talented, lovable people.
3. Accept that other people are often misguided or ill-informed, and can be safely ignored.
4. Stop feeling like a fraud and feel fabulous instead.
5. Check the facts.
6. Go into the future and take a look around.

7. Allow ourselves to be flexible in the face of knock-backs.
8. Review all of the above and change our self-talk.

TOP TIP
Think About Your Self-Talk
What do you really say to yourself?
Who could you talk to to begin making a shift?
What positive words can you include in your new self-talk?

AFFIRMATIONS

We can use *affirmations* to cement in our constructive self-talk.
Tick or circle the ones that have value to you:

- I can make a start without knowing the whole path (because I can keep myself safe)
- I can learn new skills and be good at them
- I can follow my heart and do what makes me happy
- I can change my life to suit my needs
- I can make mistakes and learn from them
- I can ask people for help with tasks
- I can think and feel at the same time
- I can pause and reflect
- I can find a way that works for me
- I can share my dreams and enlist supporters
- I can love myself and take care of my needs
- I can have ambitions and can take steps to achieve them
- I can know that my physis and my intuition are there to support and guide me
- I can take time to think
- I can go gently on myself

- I can know that I'm full of potential
- I can take pride in each step taken on my journey
- I can know that sometimes the smallest steps have the biggest impact
- I can enjoy my success
- I can rest on the way
- I can stop or change direction
- I can be active and get support when needed
- I am me
- I can live my life
- I _____ (write your own)
- I _____ (write your own)

THE PHYSIS FLOW METER

Have a look at the physis flow meter below and score yourself for where you are this week. Draw the needle where you feel you are now and then in the box underneath write in one thing that you will do to increase (or maintain) the flow of physis:

> In order to maintain or increase the flow of physis I am going to:
>
> _____
>
> _____

Chapter 8 – Doing Feelings

THE TRUTH ABOUT FEELINGS

People often shy away from talking about what's going on inside them, because they don't want to appear 'silly' or 'weak', even when their body language suggests that they're one large coffee away from a heart attack or a meltdown. We need to remember that:

1. Feelings won't go away if we ignore them
2. Feelings are a perfectly normal part of human behaviour
3. Feelings can't really be 'seen'
4. Feelings can influence our health
5. Feelings are there to help us
6. Feelings can be rediscovered
7. Feelings are ours

CLUES FOR WHEN WE'RE FEELING STRESSED

If we're doing any of these things then we should stop and reappraise our situation:

1. Tiredness
2. Outbursts
3. Inactivity
4. Tapping (Drumming our fingers or discreetly tapping a foot)
5. Compliance

6. Over-compensating

7. Headaches

8. New behaviour

9. Saying *No* or *But*

THE TWO-STAGE ANGER ATTACK

The two-stage anger attack is so named because we have two tasks to complete in order to effectively harness our anger by attacking it head-on.

STAGE ONE – DEALING WITH 'SURFACE' ANGER

- Go for a run.
- Walk briskly for as long as we need to.
- Play tennis or squash (where we can really smash the ball about).
- Scribble really hard on a pad of paper.
- Smack a punch bag.
- Go the gym and work out.
- Throw eggs against a wall.

STAGE TWO – DEALING WITH 'DEEP' ANGER

- Complete a tough piece of work that we have been delaying.
- Spend a week really focussing on establishing our next business or getting our job-hunting programme fully established.
- Work on a cherished project that we never had the time for before.

- Set a tough deadline to finish decorating the house or fixing our car.
- Enter a competition and work methodically to ensure we do well in it.

TRANSITION FEELINGS

We can add to the High-Cs model from the earlier chapter and think about what sort of feelings we are likely to experience in each stage.

TRANSITION STAGE	KEY ACTIVITY	LIKELY FEELINGS
1) Stressful Chaos	The bad stuff is happening right now!	Fear (scare) as we need to take care of ourselves
2) Tense Calm	It's over. Something has gone, been lost or changed	Relief (happy) that it's over, mixed with anxiety (scare) at what might follow and longing (sadness) at what might have been
3) Free Cleansing	Letting go of the past and tidying up our world	Cross (anger) at the way we were treated, mixed with pleasure (happy) at letting go of baggage

4) Anxious Consideration	Fact-finding and planning, thinking about consequences	Nervous (scare) at the uncertainty of the future
5) Hopeful Catching	Beginning the next stage of our modern career	Anxiety (scare) at what is to come, blended with frustration (anger) at wanting to reach a new goal. Possibly some excitement too (happy) as we're finally heading off in a new direction
6) Careful Coordination	Making progress and adjusting our course	Anxiety (scare) over whether we're heading in the right direction
7) Joyful Celebration	Celebrating progress made and way-points ticked off	Content and relaxed (happy) that we have really done well and have either bounced back, or are beginning to achieve a significant change in our fortunes

Chapter 9 – Buying Time

REDUCING STRESS

We need reduce our stress levels by extending our time horizons and we can do this by conserving our cash and planning our expenditure carefully.

THINKING ABOUT MONEY

1. How much do you have in savings?
2. What other liquid assets (cash) can you get hold of?
3. How much money will you receive from your ex-employer?
4. What can you do to take a mortgage payment holiday (with the permission of the bank)?
5. How much is owed on your credit card?
6. What non-essential expenditure can you immediately stop/ delay/reduce?
7. What else can you reduce/replace/cut in order to run your household at an absolute minimum for three months?
8. What shopping/lifestyle habits need to change to support this period?
9. Who else can you ask for support, in case of an emergency?
10. What other 'unthinkable' options are helpful to think about now?

HOW MUCH TIME DO WE NEED TO BUY?

The answer is, sadly, always more than we think we need. Have a look at the timetable and see where you fit in and how it compares to your initial estimate and financial reality:

(A) TAKING TIME TO FIND A JOB	(B) TAKING TIME TO BUILD A BUSINESS
• 0 – 3 months, if we're exceptionally well connected. • 3 – 6 months if we're exceptionally proactive and network like our life depends on it. • 6 – 12 months for the general population who seek job-hunting support. • 6 – 18 months for the general population who just trust to luck and who have no particular job-hunting skills. • 12 – 18 months for people who are hit hard by the loss of their previous role and despite good intentions, struggle to get moving for the first 6 months.	• 0 – 6 months to find a small piece of consultancy work or short interim position, if our specialisation is in demand and we go networking. • 6 – 12 months to find a consultancy contract or to begin selling products/services through our trading business. • 12 – 24 months to break even if we are running a new start-up business. • 24 – 36 months to begin generating a small profit in our start-up business.

FORWARD-LOOKING CASH MANAGEMENT

In order to make sure that we have *what* we need *when* we need it, I strongly suggest producing a cashflow forecast, which shows what our financial life will look like over the next few months, so that we don't inadvertently run out of money.

SAMPLE (A) – INITIAL CASH FLOW FORECAST

Month	Jan	Feb	Mar	Apr	May	Jun	Jul
Opening Bank Balance	0	2,250	1,000	250	-500	-1,250	-2,500
INCOME							
Redundancy payment	+2,000						
Withdraw savings	+1,500						
Planned casual work			+500	+500	+500		
EXPENSES							
Mortgage	-500	-500	-500	-500	-500	-500	-500
Food	-400	-400	-400	-400	-400	-400	-400
General household	-200	-200	-200	-200	-200	-200	-200
Taxes and utilities	-150	-150	-150	-150	-150	-150	-150
Closing Bank Balance	2,250	1,000	250	-500	-1,250	-2,500	-3,750

We can be ruthless with our expenditure and realistic about our income in order to extend our time horizon. Take a look at Sample (B) on the next page and compare it with Sample (A). What differences do you notice?

SAMPLE (B) – RUTHLESS CASH FLOW FORECAST

Month	Jan	Feb	Mar	Apr	May	Jun	Jul
Opening Bank Balance	0	2,950	2,400	1,850	1,450	1,050	650
INCOME							
Redundancy payment	+2,000						
Withdraw savings	+1,500						
Planned casual work				+150	+150	+150	Job!
EXPENSES							
Mortgage	-100	-100	-100	-100	-100	-100	-100
Food	-200	-200	-200	-200	-200	-200	-200
General household	-100	-100	-100	-100	-100	-100	-100
Taxes and utilities	-150	-150	-150	-150	-150	-150	-150
Closing Bank Balance	2,950	2,400	1,850	1,450	1,050	650	100

Chapter 10 – Thinking ABC

CREATING OPTIONS

We can create new options for ourselves by taking the time to think about it. This is often easiest when working with a supporter, coach, mentor, partner, friend – anyone who will listen to us and give us the space to develop our ideas and who will prod us by asking:

- What else could we do?
- What are all the options available to us, however silly they might sound at first?
- What do other people already do?

- What is our secret wish, dream or ambition?
- If we sat with a blank piece of paper what else might we come up with?

THE IDEAS CLOCK

When generating more options we can use a clock-face approach to get a good breadth and depth of ideas and to encourage us to be more creative.

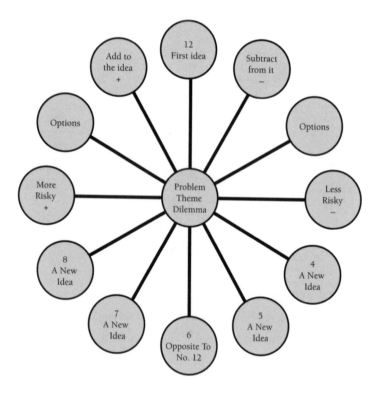

WORKED EXAMPLE FOR MY BUSINESS START-UP

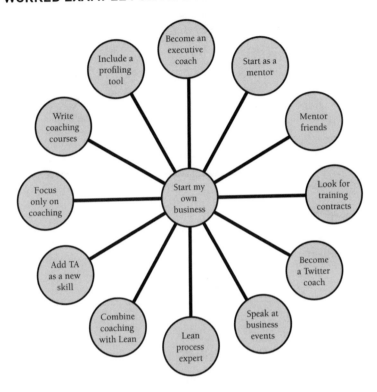

THE FACET PROCESS FOR GOOD DECISION MAKING

Good processes deliver great results and the FACET Process comprises five stages:

1. Find Facts
2. Analyse Results
3. Conclude Research
4. Evaluate Impact
5. Take Decisions

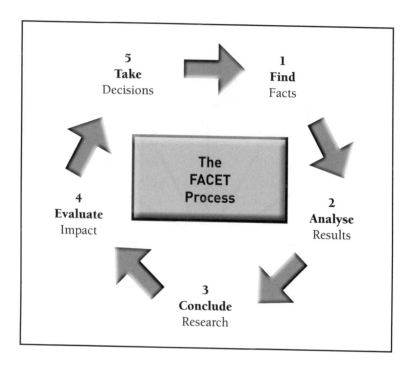

AIM FOR GROUNDED THINKING

Here are the more common bugbears that get in the way of grounded, rational, fact-based thinking and decision-making. Which ones do you do?

1. Impulsive enthusiasm
2. Rebellion
3. Influence from others
4. Hasty thinking
5. Archaeology

Chapter 11 – What's The Opportunity?

HOW TO CREATE OPPORTUNITIES

In order to bounce back we need to create new opportunities and here are ten ways to do so:

1. Increase the number of contacts we have
2. Talk to people
3. Ask for something
4. Listen to others
5. Say 'Yes'
6. Read trade magazines
7. Update our profile
8. Visit exhibitions
9. Join a networking group
10. Make an offer

WHAT ARE WE ATTRACTED TO?

To work out what particular opportunities we're attracted to we can take stock of our key skills, reflect on the people whose work interests us and consider general aspects of work that we find enjoyable. Take a moment to write a few points in the table on the following page and start to get a sense of where new opportunities might be waiting for you:

SKILL AUDIT TABLE

(1) Key work-related skills and areas of expertise	(2) Other trades or businesses that we find interesting	(3) General aspects of work that engage us and that we enjoy doing
Example: 1. Leadership expert 2. Sales skills	Example: 1. Friend who runs a flower shop 2. Colleague who retrained as a school teacher	Example: 1. Working with numbers 2. Thinking deeply to solve problems
Your skills: 1. 2. 3. 4. 5.	Other people: 1. 2. 3. 4. 5.	Your preferences: 1. 2. 3. 4. 5.

BRAND 'ME'

What is your brand? How would your friends describe you in three words? Have a look at the table on the following page and circle three words that best describe you:

3-WORD BRAND

Expert	Diligent	Practical	Punctual
Numerate	Confident	Articulate	Adaptable
Accommodating	Resilient	Driven	Caring
Ethical	Tough	Skilled	Polite
Personable	Proactive	Friendly	Reliable
Resourceful	Smart	Playful	Assertive
Incisive	Creative	Outgoing	Empathetic

MY PERSONAL BRAND IN THREE WORDS IS:		

Chapter 12 – Sales Secrets

SELLING IS ESSENTIAL

When we're actually out selling to people, we need to remember that:

- Without anybody selling anything to anyone the world order would collapse.
- We have a right to try and sell good things to good people.
- We can sell great products and services that we believe in.
- We can learn what to do and how to do it (because sales people are not born – they're made).
- We can be nervous and still excel at the same time.
- We all need to value our time and our products and services.
- We all need to value our skills and strengths.
- We can be a competent sales person and that's good enough.

SECRETS OF SUCCESS

We can be great at selling. We can do all of these things really well.

- ✓ Listen
- ✓ Turn a hard sell into an easy buy
- ✓ Speak to people
- ✓ Maintain a ratio of 6:1
- ✓ Manage our pipeline
- ✓ Mine our contacts
- ✓ Track our process
- ✓ Have tiered products
- ✓ Ask for the order
- ✓ Keep going

SIX-MONTH SALES PROCESS

It can take six months to secure new business or to find a job and if we follow a process we will increase our chances of success:

To find a new client	STAGE	To find a new job
Research organisations and networking groups where potential clients might be found	1	Research advertisements and cold call opportunities
Send introductory letters and visit networking group	2	Send out introductory letters and apply for roles
Follow-up call to arrange an introductory meeting	3	Follow up to show interest
Meet and find out about the other person, listen and think about how we could help them	4	Receive an invitation to a first interview or assessment centre

Follow up with a letter and offer possible solutions	5	Follow up to thank them for seeing you
Call to arrange a second meeting	6	Invited to attend a second interview
Meet them again and talk through our 'easy buy' for them	7	Follow up to thank them again
Ask for the order	8	Be made an offer
Receive the order	9	Consider the offer
Sign and celebrate	10	Sign and celebrate

SALES TRACKER

A sales tracker spreadsheet is a great way to make sure that we don't lose sight of new opportunities. Here is a simple example based on a fictitious building supplies business:

SALES TRACKER FOR BISHOP'S BULK BUILDING SUPPLIES LTD

Client	Opportunity	Pipeline Stage	Action Date	Action Task
Hewitt Ltd	Nails £500	3	Jan	Arrange 1st meeting
Daniels LLP	Scaffolding £2,500	3	Feb	Arrange 1st meeting
Merritt Co	Safety hats £750	5	Jan	Email options
Holmes Corp	Paint £450	6	Mar	Arrange 2nd meeting

Forrest Partners	Screws £300	3	Feb	Arrange 1st meeting
King Plc	Wood £6,000	7/8	Jan	Deliver presentation
Todd & Sons	Hammers £100	2	Feb	Send brochure

Chapter 13 – Embracing Social Media

SOCIAL MEDIA MAKES A DIFFERENCE

We can embrace the world of social media and use it to our advantage.

> **TOP TIP**
> Go where your clients live.
> If they live in the social media space then we need to as well, or we could easily lose out to a competitor.

CHOOSE YOUR PLATFORMS

There are many platforms available to us, including *Facebook*, *LinkedIn* and *Twitter*. Choose the ones that work for you and spend time on them each day, making new friends and having conversations.

TOP TEN TWITTER TIPS – GETTING STARTED

Twitter is fast, accessible and responsive. We can use it to build our network, sell products and services and tell the world that we exist. Here's how to get started:

1. Give yourself a catchy name
2. Use a smiley photo of ourselves
3. If our account is for business then leave it unlocked
4. If our account is for personal networking we might decide to lock it
5. Follow a mixture of men and women
6. Don't moan too much
7. Don't retweet too much
8. Start by going on at different times of the day
9. Don't just trust anyone
10. Beware of spam

TOP TEN TWITTER TIPS – HOW TO TWEET

Twitter allows us to send serious messages, have fun, post links, share photographs and ask questions. Follow a friend you trust and observe how they talk to people. Here are ten other ways to get tweeting:

1. Say hello and ask people how their day is going
2. Ask a specific question
3. Ask for help
4. Tell people what you're doing
5. Respond to comments about TV shows
6. Tweet a picture
7. Talk about your hobby
8. 'Make' toast
9. Use *hashtags*
10. Respond to other tweets

USING TWITTER TO SELL

We can use twitter to boost sales and create new opportunities by:

- Inviting people to read our blog.
- Inviting people to visit our LinkedIn profile.
- Inviting people to visit our Facebook fan page.
- Inviting people for a 'tweetup', where you meet for a coffee and a chat. This is a good way to cement friendships or get to know possible clients.
- Publicising our business website.
- Advertising specific products or events, with a link to a website for more information.
- Telling people what we do and inviting them to contact us.
- Using scheduled tweets to make sure that our interesting invitations or links appear in the timeline at specific points in the day.
- Using a third-party app such as Hootsuite or Tweetdeck to manage our Twitter account and create lists of potential customers. We can say hello to these people and draw their attention to a product or service.

Chapter 14 – Make a Change

7 QUOTES ON LEARNING

Here are seven useful quotes for us to reflect on:

1. We can choose whether to stay stuck or to bounce back.

2. We need to keep learning in order to bounce back.

3. If we learn nothing new, we won't know what to change.

4. If we change nothing, we will get nowhere.

5. We need to apply our learning to practical action.

6. When we make a change, we move a step forward.

7. Each new step is worth celebrating.

AND FINALLY...

If we keep going, life will improve and we *will* bounce back.

Helpful Habits
– Simple things to guide our development –

SUMMARY OF HABITS

If we create new habits for ourselves to follow we can ensure that we're doing positive things to help ourselves bounce back. Here are the helpful habits from each of the chapters in the book:

CHAPTER 1 – BOUNCING BACK FOR REAL

- Make sure we have some working time *and* some leisure time each week. The combination works in harmony to improve our thinking, creates new opportunities to meet interesting people and increases our confidence. Our aim is to achieve a happy work-life *imbalance* because that is easier to maintain.

CHAPTER 2 – MODERN CAREERS

- Keep an open mind. We might feel overwhelmed by the choices before us and the fear that our next job almost certainly won't be our last. However, if we keep an open mind and consider each option on its merit we will create useful career-enhancing opportunities for ourselves.

CHAPTER 3 – THE GYROSCOPE

- Be objective about our situation and use appropriate language. For example, if we say 'I can't do anything' that is literally not true – we can all do *something*. Instead we can say 'I can do this and with support I could do that as well'.

CHAPTER 4 – THE ESSENCE OF SUCCESS

- Keep our favourite rules in sight, so that we can be reminded of simple secrets to help us make progress. Write them on a piece of paper and stick them up somewhere that we will see them on a regular basis.

CHAPTER 5 – GETTING STARTED

- Notice when we are inactive and consider what might be causing it. We can then decide to be proactive and take an easy step forward, so that we keep making steady progress to bounce back.

CHAPTER 6 – THE HIGH-Cs TRANSITION MODEL

- Know where we are and what we're doing to progress toward the next stage. We need to be aware of our progress and to make sure that we're taking positive steps to a brighter future.

CHAPTER 7 – PHYSIS

- Keep a sharp eye on our personal physis flow meter. If we do things that increase the flow, such as getting support

from others and changing our self-talk, then we will be
enabling our physis to keep us developing.

CHAPTER 8 – DOING FEELINGS

- Notice the signs that we have a feeling lurking inside us.
  Perhaps we are snappy, or overly tired, or are resisting an
  invitation that could help us. If we notice our external
  behaviour, we can deal with what is happening inside us
  and take steps to work with our feelings for our benefit.

CHAPTER 9 – BUYING TIME

- Produce a cashflow forecast so that we can plan our income
  and expenditure for the next few months ahead, to help
  us stretch our resources as far as we can. However, simply
  'having' a cashflow forecast isn't enough – we need to
  update it each month and make sure we only spend within
  our budget.

CHAPTER 10 – THINKING ABC

- Celebrate the time we spend thinking as *productive* time.
  If we share the results of our deliberations with others and
  show them our notes they will know we have been using
  our time wisely and will encourage us to do even more
  thinking. And remember – we do have pause our thinking
  eventually and take proactive decisions.

CHAPTER 11 – WHAT'S THE OPPORTUNITY?

- Become adept at noticing when our intuition spots an
  opportunity, so that we can act on it promptly.

CHAPTER 12 – SALES SECRETS

- Keep talking to people about our products or services, so that our sales pipeline remains topped up and opportunities for new business continue to flow through.

CHAPTER 13 – EMBRACING SOCIAL MEDIA

- Choose a major social media platforms and spend some time in that space every day. We can increase our network, talk to people, share thoughts and ideas, have fun and explore all the related services on offer.

CHAPTER 14 – MAKE A CHANGE

- Keep learning something new each week so that we keep on making changes to our world, and in doing so, continue to take safe steps forward.

Other Books by Richard Maun

If you have a job, would you like to keep it? In these difficult and unstable times, the answer is most likely to be a resounding YES! This book reveals the secrets of keeping your job. It cuts to the heart of modern working life and examines the big things that trip people up and what you need to know in order to survive – because you need more than just technical skills to stay employed. You need to know how to become an added value employee.

Based on first-hand experiences of coaching people to keep their job, packed with practical tips and simple to apply, the content is designed to enable people to excel in their workplace.

How To Keep Your Job is an easy-to-read, highly practical manual for success that every modern worker needs to have if they want to reduce their stress, increase their skills and add more value, in order to stay employed and keep the money rolling in!

The secrets and skills contained in this book can make a life-changing difference to your job-hunting activities, because they are based on real-world experience and have been used by real people to get real jobs.

Packed with practical tips, essential tools, detailed examples and revealing the three big secrets of success, *Job Hunting 3.0* can accelerate you past the rest of your competitors and into a winning position.

To be successful in the modern world we need to know how

to package our talents, how to unearth opportunities and how to assert ourselves when it matters. We need to be able to build rapport with people, talk fluently about how we can add value and be agile with our thinking in order to maximise our core strengths. We also need to use technology to our advantage and embrace the new wave of social media opportunities. Moreover, *Job Hunting 3.0* is built on process thinking, because job hunting is a sales *process* and if you set up and follow a good process, you will create opportunities for positive outcomes.

In this book you will learn about the essential elements of job hunting in the modern age, including the three-horse race, the Minute To Win It, the STAR answering technique, the demons model, the 20+ places where you can look for work, performance ratios, using numbers effectively to add value to your CV, killer questions, winning at assessment centres, the pause button, aces high and the 5-slide formula.

Job Hunting 3.0 takes us through all of these elements and more, with one goal in mind: to get you ahead of the competition so that you can secure your next job.

. . . .

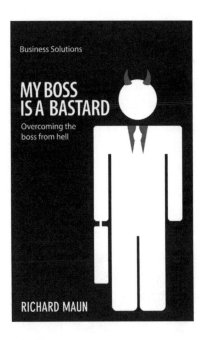

Business Solutions

MY BOSS IS A BASTARD

Overcoming the boss from hell

RICHARD MAUN

Do you have a reasonable, competent, fair-minded and even-tempered boss? Congratulations! You need read no further.

Still with us? Then you are probably one of the vast majority who have problems with your manager. He or she may be difficult, temperamental, even downright brutal, but for the sake of your career (and your sanity), you have to achieve some kind of working relationship. That's where *My Boss is a Bastard* comes in.

With a compelling blend of insight, wit and candour, Richard Maun dissects the personality types that make bad bosses and offers practical tips to help you survive everyday encounters with the monster in your office. Forewarned is forearmed: once you have recognised the raw animal nature that lurks beneath that plausible professional exterior – is it lion? Elephant? Crocodile? Or even meerkat? – you'll be better equipped to escape unscathed from your next brush with the boss. That way, you can make sure that you don't inflict on others the miseries you've had inflicted on you.

This book offers a lifeline for anyone suffering from a hostile work environment, and can help you transform the way you communicate and interact with others. It also contains a useful Personal Survival Kit, designed to help you really think about where you are and then take positive steps towards a happier, brighter and bastard-free future.

. . . .

LEAVE THE B@$T@*DS BEHIND

An Insider's Guide to Working for Yourself

Richard Maun

Ever thought of working for yourself? Of course you have – and all the time! This is the book you wish you had ten years ago.

For many people, working for themselves is something that

they yearn for and dream about. You've worked for other people's companies and been bossed around by terrible bosses for years. The time has now come to work for the best boss you could have – i.e., yourself.

This book is a straightforward, lively guide to the realities of setting up your own business, written from first-hand experience. Share in the disaster of the author's first sales meeting. Laugh at the attempts to design a business card, and wince at the pace of learning required to stay one step ahead of clients. Through such experiences, the author reveals the secrets of developing a client base and the skills which will help you through the door to self-employment in all its bare-knuckle glory. Working for yourself is one of the richest experiences in life. This practical and inspirational book will put you on the road to success.

About the Author

Richard Maun is an international career turnaround specialist, lively conference speaker and engaging workshop facilitator. He combines Transactional Analysis in organisational settings with Lean thinking, practical operational experience and his own unique career management models. His executive coaching work has been described as 'powerful' and 'genuinely transformative' and his books have been translated across the world.

Richard now runs his own management development company and is a director of a training company as well as a visiting lecturer at a leading UK university. He also works as a freelance business writer and has published four books with Marshall Cavendish – *How to Keep Your Job*, *Job Hunting 3.0*, *My Boss is a Bastard* and *Leave The B@$T@*DS Behind* – that look at how to increase performance and keep the money rolling in, how to get a job in a competitive world, how to survive turmoil at work and how to set oneself up in business. All are based on real-life experiences and contain practical tips and engaging stories.

For more information and free downloads, please visit Richard's blog site. If you would like Richard to speak at your event please contact him directly.

RICHARD CAN BE CONTACTED VIA:

Blog site:	www.richardmaun.com
LinkedIn:	Richard Maun
Twitter:	@RichardMaun
Business:	www.primarypeople.co.uk